Down the Garden Path: The Artist's Garden After Modernism

This catalogue was published on the occasion of the exhibition
"Down the Garden Path: The Artist's Garden After Modernism"
at the Queens Museum of Art, June 26–October 9, 2005

"Down the Garden Path: The Artist's Garden After Modernism" is made possible by an Emily Hall Tremaine Exhibition Award. The Exhibition Award program was founded in 1998 to honor Emily Hall Tremaine. It rewards innovation and experimentation among curators by supporting thematic exhibitions that challenge audiences and expand the boundaries of contemporary art. Additional funding is provided by the National Endowment for the Arts, the New York State Council on the Arts, Furthermore…a program of the J. M. Kaplan Fund, and The Florence Gould Foundation.

The Queens Museum of Art is housed in the New York City Building, which is owned by the City of New York. With the assistance of Queens Borough President Helen Marshall and the New York City Council, the Museum is supported in part by public funds from the New York City Department of Cultural Affairs, the New York City Department for the Aging, and the New York City Department of Youth and Community Development. Additional funding is provided by the New York State Legislature, the New York State Council on the Arts, the New York Council on the Humanities, the National Endowment for the Arts, the Institute for Museum and Library Services, and major funders:

Agnes Gund and Daniel Shapiro
Altria Group, Incorporated
Arts and Business Council
American Express Philanthropic
  Program
Carnegie Corporation of New York
The Dominick and Rose Ciampa
  Foundation
Citigroup
Deutsche Bank of the Americas
  Foundation
Emigrant Savings Bank
Ford Foundation

Goldman Sachs
The Greenwall Foundation
The Hearst Foundation
HBJ Investments, LLC
Independence Community Foundation
Furthermore…a program of the
  J. M. Kaplan Fund
JP Morgan Chase
Lily Auchincloss Foundation, Inc.
Museum Loan Network
New York Community Trust
Peter Norton Family Foundation
The Peninsula Foundation

Pickman Foundation
Richmond County Savings
  Foundation
Rockefeller Brothers Fund, Inc.
The Roslyn Savings Foundation
Silvercup Studios
The Emily Hall Tremaine
  Foundation
UBS
Verizon Foundation

Friends and members of the
  Queens Museum of Art

© 2005 Queens Museum of Art
Queens Museum of Art
New York City Building
Queens, New York 11368
www.queensmuseum.org

ISBN 1-929641-06-0

Editors: Valerie Smith, Domenick Ammirati, Jennifer Liese

Design: Omnivore/Alice Chung and Karen Hsu
Typeface: Galaxie Polaris
Stock: 130g Munken Natural text and 300g Munken Pure cover
Printed in Iceland by Oddi Printing

Cover: Paula Hayes, *Teardrop Terrarium*, 2004. Hand-blown glass with custom plantings, 12 x 26 x 11 inches. Courtesy of the artist. Photo: Eva Heyd.
Flaps: Paula Hayes, *Teardrop Terrarium*, 2004. Hand-blown glass with custom plantings, 13 x 28 x 11 inches. Courtesy of the artist. Photo: Eva Heyd.

Acknowledgments

I had wanted to do an exhibition on gardens by artists for at least eight years, well before I began working at the Queens Museum of Art. The idea evolved. Early on it was broad and all-encompassing; it touched on front yards, backyards, graveyards, courtyards, schoolyards, and junkyards. Then the dichotomy between the ideal garden and real ones crept into my thinking, along with reflections on memorials, and the contradictions inherent in notions of paradise; I saw parallels between threats to ecology and to people's private idylls. The exhibition that eventually resulted, "Down the Garden Path: The Artist's Garden After Modernism," is not by any means exhaustive. I would like to think of it as a single take on recent garden history that should inspire other interpretations and future experiments.

This exhibition would not have been at all possible without the recognition and support of the Emily Hall Tremaine Exhibition Award, which I received in 2002. I am grateful to Stewart J. Hudson, President, and Nicole E. Chevalier, Program Associate, of the Emily Hall Tremaine Foundation for their interest in coming to visit us in Queens, as well as the anonymous jurors on their Exhibitions Award Committee for choosing "Down the Garden Path" to receive the award. Soon thereafter, the National Endowment for the Arts came forward with generous support that opened up greater possibilities for us. Early on, we received a planning grant from the New York State Council on the Arts. Special funding for specific projects came from the Florence Gould Foundation, for the work of Thierry De Cordier; and from Furthermore . . . a program of the J. M. Kaplan Fund, for this exhibition catalogue.

An important segment of "Down the Garden Path" are the outdoor gardens created for it. Our request for qualification drew approximately 200 applications. From these 200, we narrowed the field to roughly 60, and then from 60 to 10. These ten artists met our request for proposal, and five were chosen. We are grateful to all the artists who participated in this process, and to the jurors: Estelle Cooper, Assistant Commissioner of Queens Parks; Bill Gotthelf, Queens Parks Designer; Jennifer Ward Souder, Director of Capital Projects/Assistant Director, Queens Botanical Garden; Mel Chin, artist; and Tom Eccles, Executive Director of the Public Art Fund. I thank them all for meeting twice and for their willingness to go through the challenging review process with Tom Finkelpearl, Executive Director of the QMA, and myself. Key to the success of the new garden projects has been the cooperation of Dorothy Lewandowski, Borough Commissioner of Queens Parks and Recreation, and Susan LeCerte, Executive Director, Queens Botanical Garden. For invaluable advice, tips on plants and distributors, and tireless trips to possible garden sites in Flushing, I owe a special thanks to Frank Colella, Principal Queens Park Supervisor.

A big thank you goes to the many authors and artists who contributed to the exhibition catalogue. Joachim Wolschke-Bulmahn's insightful essay and dazzling scholarship is a cornerstone of the book; his specialty, gardens during the Weimar Republic, partially inspired the section "Hell: The Memorial." Brigitte Franzen has written her own book on the garden in contemporary art, *Die vierte Natur* (The Fourth Nature), as-yet untranslated into English; she was an obvious choice to write an essay on this subject. Julian Agyeman has written extensively on prejudice and the environment and kindly agreed to rework an article of his on "alien species." His research on British history with regard to horticulture is a great compliment to Wolschke-Bulmahn's essay. Jamaica Kincaid's *My Garden (Book):* made a strong impression on me, as did her passionate perspective on gardens and their often dark history, so I was thrilled she agreed to write a new piece for us.

Sergio Vega's contribution on *Modernismo Tropical* and Robert Williams's on Mark Dion's *Tasting Garden* are both texts that were reworked, and we are pleased to publish them for the first time here. Thierry De Cordier's "Some Garden Writings 1991–1994" and Paul Geerts's article on Jan Vercruysse's *Labyrinth & Pleasure Gardens* are two texts that have been partially revised and newly translated into English; it is a pleasure to have them included. A special acknowledgment goes to translators Frank Albers and Bernard Dewulf for their work on De Cordier and Claude de France for her translation of Paul Geerts's text. Also included in the catalogue are two interviews I did, with Alan Sonfist and with Brian Tolle and Diana Balmori; thank you to those interviewees for their candor in conversation and their patience in reviewing and refining the transcripts; special thanks to Rachel Schuder for her speedy transcriptions.

Jennifer Liese is a wonderful editor recommended to me by Sina Najafi, who is to be thanked for this tip and also for his kindness in sharing with me his initial list of garden writers and his enthusiasm for the project. Jennifer whipped my unwieldy text into the readable one it is now; I am eternally grateful. Domenick Ammirati, who has done all the copy editing, was recommended by Jennifer and has been a tremendous help in this mammoth job; we could not have done it without his cheerful expertise. Ari Hiroshige, QMA Curatorial Assistant, has been a guardian angel throughout the process of putting together both the book and the exhibition. She is the best assistant this side of the Unisphere. Finally, Alice Chung and Karen Hsu, principles of Omnivore design studio, took on the book with energy and enthusiasm to create the colorful tome it is. We are all thrilled with their work.

Along the way, key people have contributed many other kinds of support that have made the exhibition and catalogue into a reality. Thanks go to Paul Rogers of 9W Gallery for his assistance with Alan Sonfist's project; Gwen F. Chanzit, Curator of Modern and Contemporary Art and the Herbert Bayer Collection and Archive at the Denver Art Museum, for her willingness to help with images and in sharing her thoughts on Bayer; Terence Riley, Philip Johnson Chief Curator of Architecture and Design at the Museum of Modern Art, New York, and Christian Larsen, Curatorial Assistant, for helping secure the loan of works by Roberto Burle Marx, and especially Fátima Gomes of Burle Marx & Cia. Ltda. in Rio de Janeiro for her patience, organization, and willingness to communicate in English. Keith Collins, Executor of the Derek Jarman Estate, has been charming and enormously helpful with facts about Derek and with the logistics of getting the work to New York. We were happy to have architect Nicholas Bunning's design drawings for Ghada Amer's *Happily Ever After*. Hassan served as our liason for the fabrication of Ghada's piece at Bacco Iron Works in Brooklyn; and the teak bench was made in Mexico. I owe a debt of gratitude to Marian Goodman for her encouragement and support and to Agnès Fierobe, Director of Galerie Marian Goodman, Paris, as well as to Katell Jaffrès and others on the staff there, for their assistance regarding the work of Thierry De Cordier. Thanks to Elaine Budin, Marian Goodman Gallery, New York, for her assistance regarding Lothar Baumgarten's installation. Many thanks go to John Angus, Director of the Storey Institute, Lancaster, England, for lending us Mark Dion's drawings; to artist Robert Williams, for preparing and coordinating the travel of those drawings and his own; to Gina Williams, Robert's wife, for taking them from Lancaster to London; and, finally, to Jaishri Abichandani for couriering them to New York. Linda Chinfen was a tremendous help with the installation details of Stan Douglas's work. Thank you to Jane Crawford, wife of the late Gordon Matta-Clark, who was kind enough to share with me her thoughts on Matta-Clark's work; and a big thanks to David Zwirner and Angela Choon, Director of David Zwirner Gallery, who helped us with borrowing Matta-Clark's drawings from the estate. I was fortunate to have Elyse Goldberg's knowledge and advice regarding Robert Smithson's work. David Nolan and Katherine Chan, Director of Nolan/Eckman Gallery, were wonderful to assist me with all aspects of Ian Hamilton Finlay's work; and Pia Simig, Ian's right hand, was nice enough to take time to come to QMA on his behalf. We were very fortunate to be able to borrow David Fischli and Peter Weiss's *Projection 1*

from the Sammlung Goetz, Munich. Markus Richgasse of Galerie Eva Presenhuber, Zurich, facilitated the loan; and Clifford Dossel, Lighting Designer and Technical Coordinator at the Baltimore Museum of Art, gave us valuable installation advice. Many thanks go to all the people of the village of Soebatsfontein, South Africa, who participated in the project organized by Till Krause and Ute Schmiedel of Galerie für Landschaftskunst, Hamburg. Thanks also go to Sabine Breitwieser, Artistic and Managing Director of the Generali Foundation, Vienna, and Doris Leutgeb, its Collections and Reference Room Manager, for their assistance regarding Dan Graham's *Corporate Arcadias*. Tumelo Mosaka, Assistant Curator at the Brooklyn Museum, helped me get in touch with Lonnie Graham; Brenda Phelps is on top of all aspects of Jenny Holzer's *Black Garden*, and her assistance is greatly appreciated. Carlos Cortés, artist and fabricator in San Antonio, and Todd Hanlon, artist's and studio assistant in New York, have been essential to the realization of Franco Mondini-Ruiz's *Thinking Green* outdoor garden project. Regarding the work of Isamu Noguchi, Bonnie Rychlak, Curator and Director of Collections at the Noguchi Museum and Sculpture Center, a friend and collaborator from the beginning, and Larry Giacoletti, Registrar, have played significant parts in making loans of Noguchi's works possible. Leslie Tonkonow first mentioned to me Alfonso Ossorio's conifer garden; while we were unable to borrow the work from the Foundation and Archive, Halley Harrisburg, Director of Michael Rosenfeld Gallery, was very encouraging and helped me with advice and information along the way. A big thank you goes to Diane Shamash, Director of Minetta Brook, for her inspirational work with artists, in particular Christian Philipp Müller, and for lending us his "Farmer Portraits." Brian Clyne has been incredible in every aspect of organizing the loan for Brian Tolle's Irish Hunger Memorial model, in advice about photographers, and in preparing the *Skid Rows* event at the Queens Botanical Garden. In addition, he has found time to work on a map for the exhibition for the commissioned gardens. Warren Holzman, mechanic extraordinaire, rigged up the truck for *Skid Rows*. Thank you also to Laticia Remauro, Henry Davis, and Patricia Quinn at the Battery Park City Authority for facilitating the loan of the model and photographs of the Irish Hunger Memorial. A special thank you goes to Brooke Alexander and his assistant Owen Houhoulis at Brooke Alexander Gallery, who was very kind to set up the occasion for us to photograph Jan Vercruysse's *Labyrinth & Pleasure Gardens* and to organize the loans of Jan's lithographs.

Thank yous go to the many organizations and people that make them function who gave us photographic rights, in many cases waiving costly fees or otherwise giving us a break: Jennifer Belt and Tim McCarthy for Burle Marx at Art Resource, Inc.; Janet Hicks and Cristin O'Keefe Aptowicz at Artists Rights Society, New York; Doris Nicholson at the Bodleian Library, Oriental Collections, University of Oxford, for the Persian garden image; Jonathan G. Silin for the Estate of Robert Giard, for images of Alfonso Ossorio's garden; Andrew Lawson and Judy at Andrew Lawson Photography in Oxford, England, for images of the work of Ian Hamilton Finlay; Adrienne Drake at Magazzino d'Arte Moderna, Rome, for that of Vedovamazzei; Paula Mazzotta at VAGA (Visual Artists and Galleries Association) for Robert Smithson; Iris A. Ranzinger, Collection Assistant, Picture Archive, Generali Foundation, Vienna, for images of Matta-Clark's and Dan Graham's work; Stan Ries, the photographer for Brian Tolle's Irish Hunger Memorial; Carole Lee, Manager for Rights and Reproductions at the Denver Art Museum, for Herbert Bayer images; Garett Ricciardi, who helped us with Vito Acconci images; Haruyoshi Ono, for his wonderful images of Burle Marx's gardens; Elizabeth Schwartz at Deitch Projects and Jasmine Levett and Natasha Roje at Gagosian Gallery, who helped with images of Ghada Amer's gardens; Wendy White and Christina Vassallo, Archivists, at David Zwirner Gallery, for reproductions of Matta-Clark's topiaries; Stephanie Dorsey at Matthew Marks Gallery, who supplied us with photographs of Fischli and Weiss's work; Michael Goodson, Archivist at the James Cohan Gallery, for images of Robert Smithson; Nicholas Knight for Mel Bochner; Eulas Pizarro at Salon 94 for Paula Hayes; Savannah Roberts and Jen Rhee at Minetta Brook for Christian Philipp Müller; Roman Mensing for photographs in Brigitte Franzen's text; Carl Riddle, Collections Management Assistant at the Noguchi Museum and Sculpture Center, who facilitated our using images of Noguchi's work; and Jenny Holzer, Nancy Holt, and Lothar Baumgarten.

All museum exhibitions require a hardy group of curatorial interns who come from near and far to do research and a lot of dirty work, like typing up lists, scanning images, etc. They work with dedication and eagerness, we could not function without them, and we are grateful that they are so willing. Thank you to Hermoine Salole, Majken Kramer Overgaard, and Claire K. Stringer, and special thanks to Lai Wa Chan for her dedication, graphic-design talent, and patience in scanning, formatting, and organizing the catalogue illustrations.

Lastly, I am grateful to have such a wonderful cura-torial staff: Hitomi Iwasaki, Associate Curator, who worked on the Fischli and Weiss loan and more; Arnold Kanarvogel, Chief Preparator, who along with Louise Weinberg did much of the framing, installing, and facilitating; Hsu-Han Shang, Registrar, who took care of the comings and goings; Ari Hiroshige, Curatorial Assistant, a night owl; as well as other talented museum colleagues: Lauren Schloss, Director of Education; Guadalupe Orjuela, Education Administrative Assistant; and Laura Groskinsky, Family and Teen Education Coordinator, have coordinated various aspects of Lonnie Graham's, Meg Webster's and Dave McKenzie and Anissa Mack's outdoor garden projects with families and kids in Queens. Doug Matlaga, artist and super-carpenter, and Lou Acquavita, Facilities Manager, worked on these outdoor gardens, and David Dean, Director of Planning and Individual Support, found us extra money and enthusiastically read my muddled catalogue texts. David Strauss, Director of Public Relations and Marketing, has been a great garden advocate and super-involved in the Tolle and Balmori *Skid Rows* performance and project at the Queens Botanical Garden. Thank you to Julie Lou, Director of Finance, for making me stay within budget and Lisa Edmondson, Business Manager and Associate Human Resources Mana-ger, who worked out the insurance details for the McKenzie/Mack garden project. And thank you to Tom Finkelpearl for lending his expertise in the RFQ and RFP process for the outdoor gardens and for being enthusiastic about the exhibition. Special thanks to everyone else in the QMA family and cheer-leading squad.

There have been many more individuals that helped realize this catalogue and exhibition; I hope they will forgive me if I have forgotten them. They should know that I appreciate their hard work.

Lastly, I would like to thank all the artists in the exhibition and many more whose work appears in the catalogue, some of whom have heard about this idea of mine since the late 1990s. It is so moving to have you all eager to participate and to present your ideas on the garden. Thank you to Vito Acconci, Arakawa + Gins, Ghada Amer, Lothar Baumgarten, Mel Bochner, Roberto Burle Marx, Tom Burr, Mel Chin, Thierry De Cordier, Mark Dion, Stan Douglas, Ian Hamilton Finlay, Peter Fischli and David Weiss, Galerie für Landschaftskunst (Till Krause and Ute Schmiedel and the village of Soebatsfontein), Dan Graham, Lonnie Graham, Paula Hayes, Jenny Holzer, Derek Jarman, Ronald Jones, Anissa Mack and Dave McKenzie, Gordon Matta-Clark, Franco Mondini-Ruiz, Isamu Noguchi, Nils Norman, Christian Philipp Müller, Ingrid Pollard, Robert Smithson, Alan Sonfist, Brian Tolle and Diana Balmori, Sergio Vega, Jan Vercruysse, and Meg Webster.

This exhibition is dedicated to Lucy and Cosmo, my sweetest flowers.

—Valerie Smith
Senior Curator and Director of Exhibitions

Director's Letter
Tom Finkelpearl

For the last three decades, the Queens Museum of Art has existed in the middle of Flushing Meadows-Corona Park. Our location's history has served as the subject of numerous exhibitions, from shows commemorating the two World's Fairs the park hosted, to ones focusing on the United Nations' presence here in the late 1940s, to celebrations of local heroes like Louis Armstrong. The park was created by Robert Moses for the 1939 World's Fair and is still referred to as "the Fairgrounds" in the traffic reports I listen to each morning. But Flushing Meadows is an essential public space for the people of Flushing and Corona—as well loved and as heavily used as Central Park in Manhattan—and one of the great pleasures of working at the museum or of visiting us in the summer months are its open spaces.

In 1992 Barbara C. Matilsky organized "Fragile Ecologies: Contemporary Artists' Interpretations and Solutions," an exhibition at the Queens Museum that took a strong remedial position regarding the environment, using Flushing Meadows—with its history as an ash dump—as the backdrop. "Down the Garden Path" is a show of actual and theoretical artists' gardens and, as the title suggests, the viewer takes a poetic journey of discovery. The exhibition leads through seven decades of creativity in the field, starting with the giants of modernism and moving through the conceptual and political artists who have employed gardens in recent years. After seeing this indoor portion, the visitor may venture into the park to see five new gardens commissioned for the occasion. "Down the Garden Path" is the brainchild of the museum's Director of Exhibitions Valerie Smith, who continues to explore ideas she began developing as director of Sonsbeek 93, a 1993 exhibition in the Netherlands of site-specific work throughout Sonsbeek park, the city of Arnhem, and its environs; and as curator of "Crossing the Line," 2001, an exhibition staged at multiple sites throughout Queens. In the spirit of those efforts, Smith's new, large-scale exhibition addresses a field of artistic practice that has never received due attention. Our galleries will be filled with videos, films, photographs, drawings, models, and sculptural installations of artists' gardens—with some plants mixed in. The five new gardens, which stretch the exhibition into the Queens Botanical Garden, exemplify and amplify the indoor works.

For some people, a museum is an oasis for the contemplation of art outside the flow of life, or a fortress that separates us from the bustle of the city. This feeling may comfort an insider, but it tends to exclude the uninitiated. At the Queens Museum, we are in the middle of a vibrant and well-used public space, and in recent years, we have made a concerted effort to become a greater part of Flushing Meadows-Corona Park. Each of the last two summers we have presented outdoor films, and we will expand the series this summer to include outdoor dance and music. We feel that opening up the museum to the park is good both for those who might have felt excluded in the past and for those more familiar with the institution who would be enriched by experiencing the energy that is contemporary Queens. "Down the Garden Path" speaks to multiple audiences inside and outside the museum, and it is with great pleasure that we present this ambitious project.

Introduction
Valerie Smith

The garden is a relatively young academic subject, one often subsumed into art history and generally considered lesser than landscape architecture, which itself has struggled to achieve its recent respectability and independence from architecture. This neglect is not surprising, since the design of the garden, rather than its meaning, has been the traditional emphasis of study. Escapist notions about gardens have also contributed to why they have not, until recently, received critical attention: The belief that life's relentless series of hurdles and shocks is stilled by the peace and tranquility of a garden is nature's little myth (there is nothing more fertile for the wishful imagination than the relentless growth of the green world). Too, the image of the garden as the exclusive domain of matronly ladies channeling dubious propriety into choices of color and style still haunts the field.

The idea that gardens have an ideology is a contentious one for garden historians; there are those who continue to imagine gardens as neutral or pure, devoid of political interests. But there are others who know gardens are cultural constructs that must be seen in broader contexts. Politics existed in the garden when Henry David Thoreau walked around Walden Pond contemplating the nastiness of encroaching industry; racism became a part of Vita Sackville-West's garden when, after traveling to the Far East, she returned to her isolationist England even more determined to keep exotics out of her yard. The potency of misconceptions about the nature of the garden makes it not only unfortunate but irresponsible to examine only their formal aspects and ignore the reasons they were created.

Numerous exhibitions about gardens and several about artists' gardens or artists' painted depictions of their gardens have lately been staged, with therapeutic intentions and life-affirming results. "Down the Garden Path: The Artist's Garden After Modernism" does not perpetuate the traditional photographic review of the layouts and flowery content of gardens as panaceas for their creators or publics; rather, the exhibition presents a selection of deeper, divergent, and at times darker positions found in both lived experience and scholarship. In this effort, "Down the Garden Path" includes more than just gardens per se, comprising a broad range of projects that refer to gardens as metaphors for or points of departure to understanding history, politics, and our relationship to nature. From the long and distinguished history of artists' gardens we present a small selection, chosen not because they are well known—in fact, several are imaginary and one has sadly been all but destroyed—but for their integrity and the uncompromising positions they take with regard to the world outside their boundaries. To cite a few divergent examples: Roberto Burle Marx made every one of his gardens an advocacy for the rain forest; Alan Sonfist's precolonial garden and Meg Webster's philosophy of green sustainability are exemplars of proposals for urban renewal; and Stan Douglas's photographs of Schreber gardens, coupled with his film *Der Sandmann*, bring a magical network of literature, psychoanalysis, and national agendas to bear on that subject.

A few arguable crossovers aside, "Down the Garden Path" is composed of artists—not landscape architects who are occasional artists, nor artists working with organic matter, but artists who create real gardens or refer to specific gardens. The exhibition begins with three second-generation modernists who have inspired a younger, postmodernist generation to make the garden central to their creative practices. Their work emanates from three different corners of the earth and spans the globe: Roberto Burle Marx lived and worked in Brazil, but his designs can be found in at least four other countries in South America, six in Europe, and several in North America and Asia. Isamu Noguchi, who brings a decidedly Eastern awareness to the exhibition, was based in Japan and New York and, like Burle Marx, left a significant international legacy. Ian Hamilton Finlay is an artist-poet whose major work is grounded in the Pentlands of Scotland and, more recently, in southern France; he brings a certain cunning to the exhibition that one might identify as Scottish and therefore from the North, yet he's firmly committed to the history and literature of the Continent. Finally, while Herbert Bayer is unfortunately not represented in the exhibition, his gardens and earthworks are included here in the catalogue. As an Austrian Bauhaus student and teacher who then emigrated to the United States, he adds another compass point to the global sketch in the following pages. We turn section by section to gardens that explore ideas about paradise; memorials; gardens for pleasure and play; and working gardens—a compilation of garden narratives that reveals the depth of meaning and the possibilities for surprising associations in this verdant corner of art.

Queens Museum of Art
Down the Garden Path

(left)
Prayer rug with war motifs,
Afghanistan, 1980s
Private collection

(right)
Paradise, late 18th century
Coarse brown paper
From A. F. L. Beeston, *Catalogue of the Persian, Turkish, Hindustani, and Pushtu Manuscripts in*

the Bodleian Library (Oxford: Clarendon Press, 1954)
Courtesy of Department of Oriental Collections, Bodleian Library, University of Oxford

{13}

Chapter 1
Heaven: Paradise
Valerie Smith

If the goal of the garden is to provide "shelter . . . from the change and contradictions we feel in relation to nature and other humans,"[1] then our impulse will be to create an idealized garden, the good garden, because the reality outside (i.e., the landscape against which we are exposed and defenseless, and the social world) is too terrifying to contemplate. And yet perversely, in order to hold our interest, a garden must entertain a conflict, which is guaranteed by the fallibility of humanity: That sense of tension was created in the first garden, paradise, when evil in the form of a snake offered the apple. The following investigations into the garden play with the idea of paradise and metaphorize such a reconciliation of opposites.

The etymology of the word "paradise" contains the idea of defense. It derives from the Old Persian *pairi-daeza*, the roots of which suggest an enclosure: *pairi* meaning "around" and *daeza* meaning "wall." Historically the Persians saw the garden as "a preserve set off (and protected) from the often-hostile landscape beyond."[2] The Greeks used the word *paradeisos* to refer to the hunting parks of the Persian kings, which were protected by fortifications. The first paradise garden was probably created by the Mesopotamians in what is current-day Iraq,[3] where the barren and dusty countryside around Baghdad uncannily resembles descriptions of Arcady, that mythological terrain poetically rendered as a verdant idyll by Virgil.[4]

The idea of a terrestrial paradise could only have been born out of relentless sun and arid soil, which necessitated a fertile retreat made possible by a simple system of irrigation. The gardens therefore often took the form of squares or rectangles divided into quadrants by four rivers, symbolizing the four corners of the earth, a sacred figure present in Persian ceramics some six thousand years ago.[5] The bilateral symmetry of paradise traveled from the East to the West through Constantinople and Spain, where this design is found again, centuries later, in medieval cloisters, with a tree or a fountain at its center as an *axis mundi*, a vertical conveyor from earth to heaven. One of the earliest representations of paradise can be seen woven into the Persian rugs that still adorn living-room floors today. In recent decades, depictions of paradise on some Afghan prayer rugs have been replaced with images of war, icons of the struggle to defend paradise against imperial power.

Centuries before recent Afghan wars, in colonial South America, Antonio de Leon Pinelo (1596–ca. 1675), a Peruvian historian raised by Jesuits in Lima, began his obsessive quest for paradise when he left for Spain in 1612 to serve as attorney and later a judge of the Council of the Indies. He wrote many books on the political, geographic, and botanical conditions of the colonies, the most famous of which was a bibliography of writings on South America published in Madrid in 1629. In his 1650 book *El paraíso en el nuevo mundo* (Paradise in the New World), Pinelo used the nascent science of natural history to prove that the Garden of Eden was in fact located in South America.[6]

Artist Sergio Vega revisited Pinelo's crusade with his *Modernismo Tropical*. This project, which he has been expanding for nearly a decade, uses text, photography, video, and architectural models to concretize the artist's journey to the site of Pinelo's Eden, now the city of Cuiabá in the state of Mato Grosso, Brazil. Roaming the streets of Cuiabá, Vega stumbles into a favela, and likens the shantytown to an abandoned Alice's Wonderland. He finds a "decrepit garden with flowers growing between garbage and building materials"[7]; suddenly, an Amazonian woman emerges from the detritus. This "maternal body" looms large against a symbolic Eden after the Fall. She hurls stones and insults; sleeping dogs come alive with barks and bite the artist, who hobbles fearfully away. In his arrogance, Vega had assumed trespassing rights in paradise, and was castigated by a larger-than-life Eve.

Vega is forced to flee to the relative security of a middle-class, modern-architecture housing development, where he has an epiphany. He describes the buildings as "strident in color and voluptuous in form . . . bizarre adaptations of Roberto Burle Marx's paradigmatic search for biomorphic archetypes." He goes on: "Maybe I was suffering from heat stroke as I ran up the hill, but those buildings seemed like a carnival parade that was dancing to the smooth sound of the *Bossa Nova* and heralding the triumph of modernity over the jungle. . . . Modernism in the tropics had abandoned Cartesian logic to take a nap and woke up later in the middle of a Shamanistic ritual, cross-dressed as an animal—or plant." Vega replaces the modernist notion of objectivity, "the neutral, archival, clinical image," with "the paranoid gaze of a Protestant deity."[8] God is a photographer/artist who revels in the Fall of Eden, a Fall his vocation helps to create.

In Vega's vision, the pursuit of art becomes a colonizing act, or a recolonizing of the failure and waste of modernist ideals: Henri Cartier-Bresson's "decisive moment," which Vega invokes, is not without consequences. Exoticism results from rarified snapshots of economic inequality for a public that goes to a specialized place to experience art. The Latinization of modernism—*Modernismo Tropical*, Vega calls it—may offer a more organic, vernacular, and jazzier version of progressive design, but it cannot disguise the ideology that created it, an ideology that widens the gap between economic classes, producing vertical shadows over the remains of what was once Pinelo's oasis. Vega's quirky postmodernist maquettes, with titles such as *Banana Building* and *Crocodilia Construct* (both 2002), take the occasion of

Queens Museum of Art
Down the Garden Path

Chapter 1
Heaven: Paradise

(clockwise from top left)
Sergio Vega
Modernismo Tropical
(detail), 2002
Digital print, 70 x 180 inches
Courtesy of the artist

Sergio Vega
Crocodilia Construct, 2002
Mixed-media model,
48 x 44 x 84 inches
Courtesy of the artist

Sergio Vega
Banana Building, 2002
Mixed-media model,
18 x 44 x 44 inches
Courtesy of the artist

Sergio Vega
*Rubens's Parrot, After
Tiziano* (detail), 1999
C-print, 16 x 20 inches
Courtesy of the artist

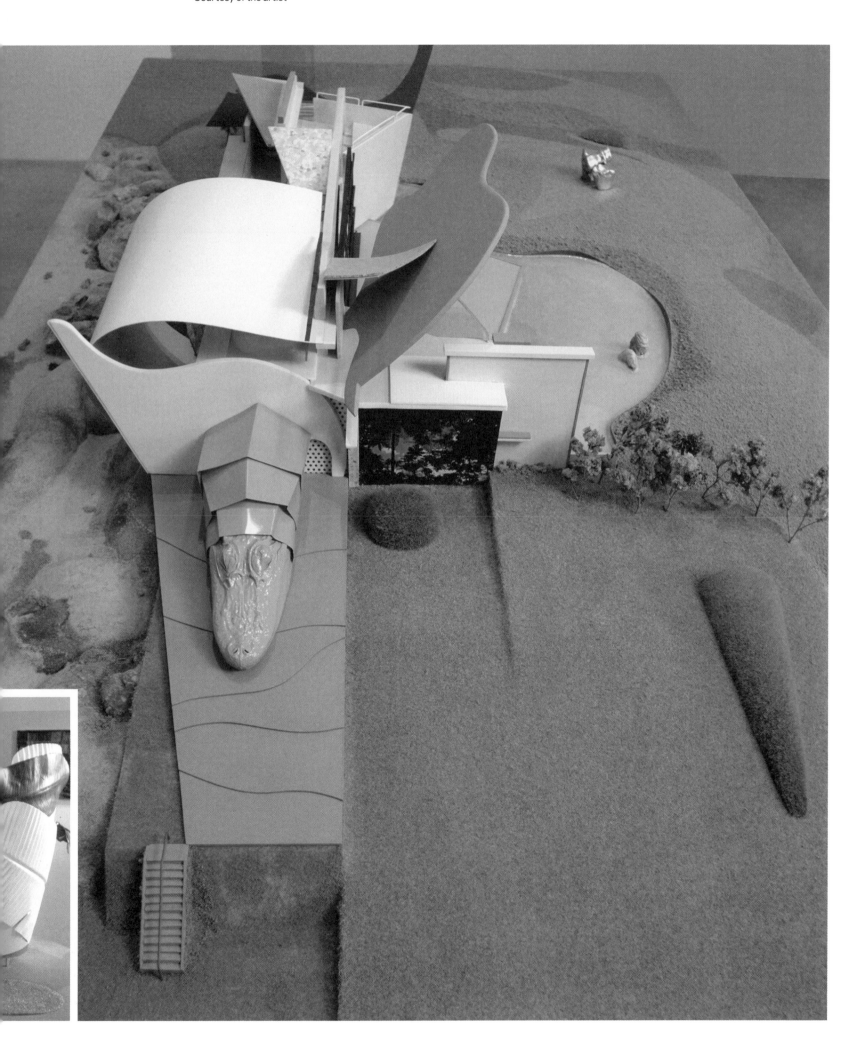

tropical architecture to turn up the volume against the sobering "structuralist study of poverty." In photographic works from 1999 to 2003, the effusive abundance of jungle aesthetics, excessive vegetation, "sunburned colors," and fermenting smells are checked by representations of military terrorism, escalating poverty, urban blight, and social decadence, reminding us that the Fall is the human condition, that paradise was lost well before Pinelo was born.

South American colonizers at the turn of the twentieth century were typically afraid of the "green hell," a rampant nature they did their best to control. In Brazil, which had been a Portuguese colony for more than three centuries, formal European design was the popular style for public gardens. Roberto Burle Marx grew up among highly structured, flowered *allés* similar to the *ramblas* of Lisbon and Madrid. Born to a German father who raised dogs and horses for a living and a Brazilian mother, a pianist of French and English descent, Burle Marx was a hybrid: a European Brazilian, educated, multilingual, and cultured. In 1928, at the height of the Weimar Republic, the Burle Marx family spent a year in Berlin. There Burle Marx learned to paint in the Expressionist style, supplementing that study of form and color with visits to the hothouses of the Dahlem Botanischer Gärten und Botanisches Museum, where he discovered the indigenous plants of his native country. The irony of traveling overseas to discover the flora of his homeland led to a lifetime of advocacy for the preservation and study of native South American plant species that were being rapidly destroyed in the rain forest. Burle Marx became a professional horticulturist and amateur botanist, keeping an extensive inventory of rare species that he propagated for his extraordinary private and public commissions.

In 1949 Burle Marx and his brother bought Santo Antônio da Bica, a *sítio*, or country property, in the mountains above Rio de Janeiro (he would later donate the place, along with his diverse collections, to the city). That same year, he began to make trips, or *coletas*,[9] into the heart of Brazil to retrieve rare and unknown species of plants.[10] It was on these *coletas* that he developed an acute sense of the symbiosis of living things, that everything had its place in the world and that cohabitation was essential to the survival of all species.

Burle Marx thought of his own garden at Santo Antônio da Bica and his commissions for private gardens as places to display, conserve, and perpetuate species that were not available on the open market and threatened in the wild. The forest was a place for him to gather specimens and knowledge of how species lived and behaved in situ. The garden, on the other hand, both had an aesthetic purpose and served as a sanctuary for endangered plants and a laboratory for their propagation. Burle Marx's mission was to give back to Brazil what it had lost during the colonial period and to overturn public complacency regarding systematic deforestation. His dual ancestry, coupled with his tremendous contribution to South American cultural identity, placed him in a perfect position to advocate for paradise with those in power. He lectured extensively on humanity's responsibility to the rain forest, and, while his pleas were not always met with action, his dedication earned him the unofficial title of the father of the ecology movement in Brazil.

Burle Marx's collections of pre-Columbian artifacts (including clay figures from Jequitinhonha), minerals, modernist art, and sacred and secular folk art informed his work with gardens in their simplicity and abstraction.

(clockwise from left)
Roberto Burle Marx
Fazenda Marambaia, 1949-54
Correas, Rio de Janeiro
Courtesy of Burle Marx & Cia. Ltda.
Photo: Haruyoshi Ono

Roberto Burle Marx
Flora da Amazônia, 1966
Ink on paper, 35 ¾ x 55 ¼ inches
Concept design for Parque
Zoobotânico de Brasília, DF,
1960-61
Courtesy of Burle Marx & Cia. Ltda.

Roberto Burle Marx
Site plan, beach house for
Mr. and Mrs. Burton Tremaine,
Santa Barbara, CA, 1948
Gouache on board,
50 ¼ x 27 ¾ inches
The Museum of Modern Art,
New York; Gift of Mrs. Burton

Tremaine (SC19.1966); Digital
image © The Museum of Modern
Art/Licensed by SCALA/Art
Resource, NY; Photo: Kate Keller

He borrowed formal ideas from modern artists including Alexander Calder, Joan Miró, and Hans Arp, all of whom exhibited and were collected in Brazil. Volumes seen from different angles, interlocked or transparent and transposed, provided structure and order that was forever shifting, and literally being shifted, as Burle Marx manipulated entire sections of his gardens to create dramatic perspectives. Plants were used relationally, for their colors and unusual forms. Burle Marx would bring back specimens from around the world, adjusting their placement in what he called "artificial ecological associations," until they reached "phytocenosis—when groupings of plants that live together in a specific place within an ecosystem reach the maximum stage of their evolution and form stable communities."[11] These horticultural juxtapositions make Burle Marx fascinating to a postmodernist generation, as does the multiplicity of his practice: painting, music, gardens. An entirely unselfconscious artist, Burle Marx transposed painting into the terms of landscape, and landscape into a process completed over time. His goal, to "decolonize the tradition of gardens in Brazil,"[12] restored one paradise to its rightful people.

Fundamental concerns about indigenous-landscape reform in Brazil, for which Burle Marx so eloquently argued in his lectures, have been echoed by many artists since. Lothar Baumgarten grew up in Düsseldorf, but his ongoing artistic concern has been to connect our contemporary experience of landscape to the way it was experienced by those who originally inhabited it. While this aspect of his work has yet to take the literal form of a garden, Baumgarten has pierced Western attitudes toward the "paradise" found in the Southern Hemisphere. At first, like Henry David Thoreau, Baumgarten demonstrated his political convictions from his own backyard. In his film *The Origin of the Night: Amazon Cosmos*, 1973–77, shots of a wasteland in the Rheinish swamps near the Düsseldorf airport were inspired by the Tupi Indian myth describing the creation of the night and the animals on earth. Then, between 1978 and 1980, Baumgarten had an opportunity to live among the Yanomami peoples in the Orinoco Basin southwest of Venezuela. *America Invention*, 1993, at the Guggenheim Museum in New York, was the culmination of work done in Europe beginning in the early 1980s. With a sequence of phonetic or Latinized inscriptions of native South American society names on walls—misnomers drawn from histories, literature, maps—the artist points to how the richly communicative language of a nonliterate people vanishes along with the rest of its culture, *especially* in the face of the elaborate cultural constructs of an invented written language.

Ingrid Pollard, a British citizen of Guyanese descent, has spent the majority of her artistic career analyzing her relationship to the British landscape. In extensive research at tourist destinations along the British coast and heritage sites inland, she seeks to find and understand her identity in places that do not acknowledge her existence: "It's as if the Black experience is only lived within an urban environment. I thought I liked the Lake District where I wandered lonely as a Black face in a sea of white. A visit to the countryside is always accompanied by a feeling of unease, dread, . . . [a] feeling I don't belong. Walks through leafy glades with a baseball bat by my side."[13] The alienation evoked in Pollard's account of her experience of historical sites in her own country can be attributed to the local governments that manage them. An absence of factual information and physical evidence

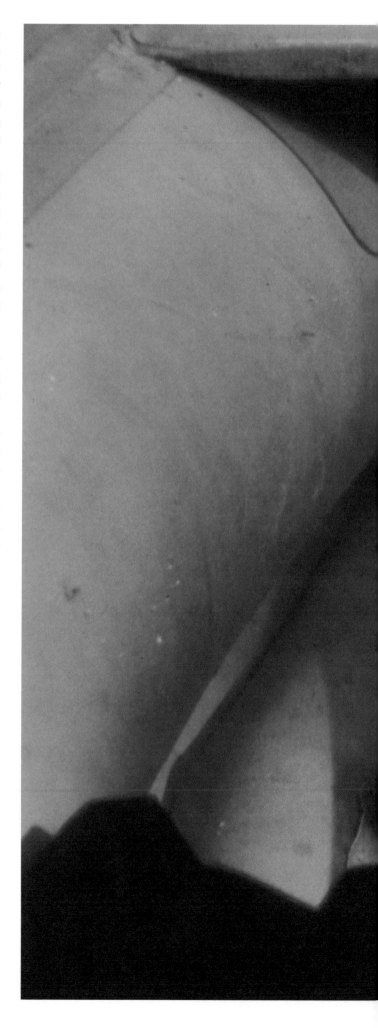

Queens Museum of Art
Down the Garden Path

Chapter 1
Heaven: Paradise

Lothar Baumgarten
El Dorado, 1970
Slide projection
From *Da gefällt's mir besser als
in Westfalen* (I Like It Here Better
Than in Westphalia), 1968–76

Queens Museum of Art
Down the Garden Path

Chapter 1
Heaven: Paradise

Lothar Baumgarten
Ant Society, 1968
Slide projection
From *Da gefällt's mir besser als
in Westfalen* (I Like It Here Better
Than in Westphalia), 1968–76

©2005 Artists Rights
Society (ARS), New York /
VG Bild-Kunst, Bonn

(inset)
Lothar Baumgarten
Anticipated Armadillo, 1970

Slide projection
From *Da gefällt's mir besser als
in Westfalen* (I Like It Here Better
Than in Westphalia), 1968–76
©2005 Artists Rights Society
(ARS), New York / VG Bild-
Kunst, Bonn

regarding the British empire's involvement in the colonies can only be read as a self-perpetuating selective history dead set on preserving a dominant political agenda.

To claim her rightful place in a land that rejects her heritage, Pollard has photographed herself, her family, and her friends amid the stark hills and trails of England, collected in her 2004 book *Postcards Home*. The photos press the psychological against the *paysage* in unsettling ways: In some, signs of industry such as telegraph pylons amid bucolic vistas with sheep grazing echo paintings by Manet, Seurat, and others, who reminded their viewers that in modern life the machine had encroached on the sanctuary of the countryside and that this was not viewed as a disruption. In her *Hidden Histories, Heritage Stories* (1994), Pollard presents sets of three photographs: the gardener, the landscape, and the tool. These triptychs have an aggressive, mug-shot quality, with menacing implements against benign bits of turf like documentary evidence of a crime. The gardeners in their working outfits are not criminals, however, but rangers who labor on the land. As Pollard writes, "They do the stuff that 'people' do in regular gardens, emotionally and physically. They just happen to work in a garden that is open to *all* people *all* the time. The 'garden' they work in is the Lee Valley National Park."[14]

Pollard makes clear in her photographic essays that gardens, parks, and landscapes have a long history that points past ownership to the people who traditionally took responsibility through manual labor for the maintenance of what have now become tourist destinations and national legacies—people who were mostly colonial slaves and their descendents. When the parks' heritage is used "to deny, cover up and sanitise the personal and community histories of a sector of British society . . . [then they] will continue to be visited by a white middle-class mirror image of those gatekeepers who manage such resources,"[15] as is still the case today.

In 1999's *My Garden (Book):*, Jamaica Kincaid discusses the restless European desire for scientific acquisition through the hierarchical system of classification known as Linnaean taxonomy, named after the famous Swedish botanist Carolus Linnaeus (1707–1778). Linnaeus, whose father Latinized his son's name to make it sound more weighty, developed binominal nomenclature to organize the numerous plant species brought to him from around the world by his students. "To name is to possess," observes Kincaid. By replacing native names with Latin names or their own family names, botanists of the Enlightenment forged a European tradition of conquering through the intellectualization of nature. They not only took pleasure in reason and order, as Kincaid proposes, but harnessed the unfathomable, giving a new structure to what they saw as structureless. With a few exceptions, the Linnaean system has largely been left unchallenged today.

Perceptions of a garden's appearance, how people speak and write about one, are telling of the observer's place in society. Kincaid notes that the rich, material way Henry James writes about a summer afternoon in the garden "could have been written only by a person who comes from a place where the wealth of the world is like a skin, a natural part of the body, a right, assumed, like having two hands and on them five fingers each."[16] Enjoying nature for its sheer beauty as a leisure activity is a world apart from utilizing plants as food and medicine. Writing about Canna lilies in South Africa, the Zimbabwean author Tsitsi Dangarembga has her young protagonist exclaim that "plants like that belonged to the cities . . . belonged to the pages of my language reader. . . . Bright and cheery, they had been

Queens Museum of Art
Down the Garden Path

Chapter 1
Heaven: Paradise

Ingrid Pollard
Hidden Histories,
Heritage Stories, 1994
Three gelatin-silver prints,
36 x 108 inches overall

{23}

planted for joy. What a strange idea that was."[17] Such a perspective will be foreign to those of us who read it in a chapter on paradise in a catalogue on the rarified subject of the artist's garden—which is all the more reason to note it in conclusion here.

NOTES

[1] Evan Eisenberg, *The Ecology of Eden* (New York: Alfred A. Knopf, 1998), 170.

[2] Sheila Blair and Jonathan Bloom, preface to the English edition, *Gardens of Iran: Ancient Wisdom, New Visions* (Tehran: Tehran Museum of Contemporary Art, 2004), 11.

[3] And probably by women who desired to settle as opposed to continue the nomadic life; see ibid., 17.

[4] Iran too claims the first paradise, located between its provinces of Ilam and Fars. Ibid., 14.

[5] The quadrant format was originally derived from the Hindu or Buddhist mandala, which divides the world into four corners. This description of heaven is similar to that which appears in the Iranian holy book the Avesta. Ibid.

[6] Pinelo also wrote a curious tome on the "moral question" of whether chocolate had ecclesiastical properties, in 1636.

[7] Sergio Vega, "Alice's Backyard," 2002, unpublished text. See also Sergio Vega, "*Modernismo Tropical*," in these pages.

[8] Sergio Vega, "*Modernismo Tropical*," 2001, unpublished text. See also Vega, "*Modernismo Tropical*."

[9] Iris Marta Montero, *Roberto Burle Marx: The Lyrical Landscape* (Berkeley and Los Angeles: University of California Press, 2001), 23. Burle Marx began making trips into the forest with his mentor Henrique Lahmeyer de Mello Barreto to stock Araxá Thermal Park with rare tropical species in 1943. For a partial list of these plants, see ibid., 54.

[10] Rossana Vaccarino, ed., *Roberto Burle Marx: Landscapes Reflected* (New York: Princeton Architectural Press with the Harvard University Graduate School of Design, 2000), 8. Marx "discovered over forty tropical plants that today bear his name" (ibid.).

[11] Montero, *Roberto Burle Marx: The Lyrical Landscape*, 24.

[12] Vaccarino, ed., *Roberto Burle Marx: Landscapes Reflected*, 28.

[13] Ingrid Pollard, *Postcards Home* (London: Chris Boot, 2004), 21.

[14] Ingrid Pollard, e-mail to the author, Oct. 19, 2004.

[15] Julian Agyeman, "Alien Species," in *Museums Journal* (December 1993): 23.

[16] Jamaica Kincaid, *My Garden (Book):* (New York: Farrar, Straus and Giroux, 1999), 116.

[17] Quoted in ibid., 115.

Hell: The Memorial

Some of the most complexly conceived and psychologically challenging gardens are those designed to commemorate. While the memorial garden is an aestheticized representation of a specific traumatic event, a war or a natural disaster, it also leverages that event by triggering the memory of other tragedies of greater or lesser importance. We may recognize aspects of our own lives and even our own actions in relation to the message of the memorial. Or our associations may be more generalized, concerned with the transgressions of humanity. The soil on which the garden is set, for instance, may remind us that whatever land we stand on was once wilderness; but as long as there's been humankind, that neutral ground has been subject to politics.

Land in relation to patrimony found a newly macabre meaning in the late-nineteenth-to-mid-twentieth-century German movement toward the nationalization of nature.[1] Not only were specific species of trees and plants chosen for their "patriotic" associations, but a primeval nature uninfluenced by foreign or formal design (such as the burial mounds or sacred groves made by "people of Nordic origin") became the ideological ideal as a site for the creation of a "pure" Teutonic people. According to historian Simon Schama, "*Germanentum*—the idea of a biologically pure and inviolate race, as 'natural' to its terrain as indigenous species of trees and flowers—featured in much of the archaeological and pre-historical literature both before and after the First World War."[2] The German idealization of a classical pagan past, dating back to Tacitus's *Germania* (a written account of the first Continental tribes of Europe, an existing copy of which was owned by Italy and coveted by Hitler),[3] dominated the search for national identity and had profound influence on the theorization of National Socialism.

The Latin aphorism *Et in Arcadia Ego* (Even in Arcady, I, Death, Hold Sway[4]) provides another powerful and oft-used classical referent for the garden memorial. The statement points to the poetic presence of mortality everywhere and lends an appropriate existential resonance to the garden. The mythological land of Arcady, where Pan roamed and music reigned, was known in ancient times as a rustic wasteland until Virgil depicted it in his *Eclogues* as a lush and verdant place where the unattainable human desire for perfection led to inevitable melancholy, an elegiac state. In the early 1620s *Et in Arcadia Ego* was reconceived as a memento mori (complete with death's-head) by Giovanni Francesco Guercino. Nicolas Poussin later interpreted the phrase in more philosophical terms, as a meditation on death in two eponymous paintings, including one famously in the Louvre.[5] While multiple variations on the presence of death in Arcady have emerged, most recognize the motto as both a warning regarding the inevitability of death and an invitation to ruminate on the possibility that immortality can be achieved through philosophy or art. Such conditions constitute the essence of the memorial.

Ian Hamilton Finlay has breathed new life into the phrase *Et in Arcadia Ego* with his recontextualizations of it in naturalized settings. He has pushed the motif across historical eras and used it to trespass against political lines, engraving it in stone above the mouth of a font that regurgitates the polluted waters of the Haagse Beek and Court Pool, and which boldly faces a public park at the seat of the European Union at The Hague (1998). It also appears in "Footnotes to an Essay" (1977), with text by Stephen Bann and images drawn by Gary Hincks according to the concept by Finlay. And he used the phrase as the title for a series of ten drawings, five after famous classical paintings by four painters on the *Et in Arcadia Ego* theme, and below them Finlay's five drawn responses in which the tomb has been replaced by a tank from the SS Panzer division and the skull by a German insignia on the tank. Finlay's iconography of death in the garden maps an evolution over two centuries; the five pairs of comparative drawings form a circular play on the moralistic and elegiac interpretations of *Et in Arcadia Ego*, only to rest with "a Romantic yearning for the classical ideal."[6] While the phrase may not be rampant among the frequently shifting constellation of monuments carefully arranged in Finlay's own garden, Stonypath/Little Sparta, in Scotland, a growing sense of warning and surprise pervades the place, underscoring his belief that "certain gardens are described as retreats when they are really attacks."[7]

Finlay also channels the creative value of violence through images of the French Revolution. Among the most impressive is a colossal gilded head of Apollo, the god of music and war, which ambushes the innocent visitor to one of Little Sparta's wooded areas, recalling the dual nature of Arcadia as home to both poets and soldiers. In art, the fragment is both a stand-in for a greater whole and a romantic reference to decay and destruction. The sudden appearance of a gigantic decapitated Apollo branded across the forehead as "*Apollon Terroriste*" immediately invokes the bloody consequences of the French Revolution, and for that matter any revolution. But Apollo's stony stare is tempered by his luxurious gold coating, a nod to the gilt and polychrome sculptures of antiquity that once conveyed a symbolic order for the French while today emphasizing his supernatural presence and simultaneously pushing his godly stature to excess; a terrorist certainly, but one who cuts a macabre impression against the leafy background and reveals Finlay's delight in the uncanny.

Finlay has experimented extensively with symbols of World War II, nestling such objects as his variations on *Lyre*, 1977, a carved image or a

Queens Museum of Art
Down the Garden Path

Chapter 1
Hell: The Memorial

(clockwise from top left)
Ian Hamilton Finlay
Submarine sculpture, n.d.
Installation view, Little Sparta,
Dunsyre, Scotland
Courtesy of Nolan/Eckman Gallery
Photo: Andrew Lawson

Ian Hamilton Finlay
(with Alexander Stoddart)
Apollon Terroriste, 1988
Resin and gold leaf
Installation view, Little Sparta,
Dunsyre, Scotland
Courtesy of Nolan/Eckman Gallery
Photo: Andrew Lawson

Ian Hamilton Finlay
(with Peter Coates)
Five Finials, 2001
Sandstone, 15 ⅓ x 8 ⅓ x
8 ⅓ inches each
Courtesy of Nolan/Eckman Gallery

metal sculpture of a Mk 2 machine gun with an inscription, comfortably within pastoral sites. While Finlay served as a sergeant in the Royal Army Service Corps and worked in Germany,[8] the use of armaments in the garden holds, in fact, a more puerile fascination for him than is immediately obvious, one that suggests the critical and assertive power of wit as a catalyst. Finlay's series of prints "Heroic Emblems" (1977) play with the emblem's ancient and Renaissance forms. A simple text or a few words in conjunction with an image of war machinery are deployed to produce metaphors with contemporary echoes. In sculptural works, often accompanied by a poetic legend, a machine gun may double as a flute and an aircraft carrier as a birdbath or fountain. The punning designs of these intentionally open-ended cartoons of military mini-monuments are imbrications of strangely humorous and serious symbols within a poetic context. They release an urgency within the landscape, with a literary and historical edge.

Jenny Holzer's 1994 *Black Garden*, a memorial set in Nordhorn, Germany, insists that the language of war is visceral and present rather than intellectual and historical. This haunting work has an involved story. On November 11, 1914, German reservists and Belgian troops fought an important battle at Langemarck, a Belgian town on the French border. Belgium had maintained neutrality until the Germans invaded to force through into France, and they were seriously disadvantaged. But poor strategy and a lack of artillery resulted in the deaths of approximately seventy thousand Germans. The German government refused to acknowledge Langemarck as a defeat, however, and the battle was "skillfully transformed into a legend about sacrifice, the sacrifice of the German troops."[9] To this end, a memorial of the battle of Langemarck was consecrated on November 24, 1929, in the German city of Nordhorn.

The memorial was to undergo several subsequent permutations. An old photograph shows the original bronze figure with a raised arm atop a base inscribed "*Metallspende des Deutschen Volkes*" (Endurance of the German People). Neither the classicism of the male nude figure nor its message of immortality could have been lost on visitors. In 1938 the site was named Langemarckplatz and became the cult center of National Socialism, "employed to prepare the Hitler Youth for their involvement in the war later on."[10] In 1940 the figure was melted down and replaced with a metal vessel similar to the Olympic torch; but the fashion for a more abstract image did not override its function as a powerful symbol of invincibility. The Nazi party further idealized Langemarck as a "victorious moment in German history when brave men voluntarily died for their Fatherland," establishing what became known as the "Langemarck Myth."

Decades later, the city of Nordhorn commissioned Holzer to reconceive the memorial in a way that would engage both World Wars. On the half-acre plot she planted rows of black flowers in four concentric circles surrounding a black apple tree. From a bird's-eye view of the garden, one sees a tree-lined clearing accessed by four entryways that cut through and diagonally divide the four circles into quarters like the crosshairs of a tactical scope on a long-range rifle. Approaching the garden from a set of ascending stairs, one gradually begins to see the formal pattern of forty-two varieties of black plants. Five benches of Bentheimer sandstone line the periphery, each bearing a chiseled statement speaking to the physicality of war:

Queens Museum of Art
Down the Garden Path

Chapter 1
Hell: The Memorial

Jenny Holzer
Black Garden, 1994
Concentric black planting with
five Bentheimer red sandstone
benches, and small white garden
Nordhorn, Germany

© 2005 Jenny Holzer
Artists Rights Society (ARS),
New York
Photos: Martin Köttering
(top left and bottom left),
Klaus Frahm (right)

BURNED ALL OVER SO ONLY HIS TEETH ARE GOOD,
HE SITS FUSED TO THE TANK.
METAL HOLDS THE BLAST HEAT AND THE SUN.
HIS DEATH IS FRESH AND THE SMELL PLEASANT.
HE MUST BE PULLED AWAY SKIN SPLITTING.
HE IS A SUGGESTION THAT AFFECTS PEOPLE DIFFERENTLY.

We enter the *Black Garden* deliberately, to be caught up by the sorrow of the memory, as if it were a necessity. The dark, slightly purple tint of the garden suggests black-and-white newsreels or vintage photos of World War II, with the vivid color of war filled in by the imagination as the visitor sits peacefully on the benches. As horrific events occur, they are reported in inexhaustible ways over time then interpreted again in as many: *Black Garden* addresses the complexities of history and how those complexities are transmitted to and treated by the public. But these issues are subsumed by a revulsion to violence and death as we internalize the image created by the words on the benches.

Some of Ronald Jones's best-known works are his numerous variations on the *Cosmic Garden*, which he has organized since 1995 with institutions throughout Europe and elsewhere. The earliest renderings of the cosmic plan are found in ancient Persian designs of paradise woven into rugs, and Islamic gardeners used the Tigris and Euphrates rivers as inspiration in dividing their paradise gardens into quadrants symbolizing the four corners of the earth. Jones's *Cosmic Garden* began with a vintage photograph from a collection of World War II images he found among his father's papers.[11] Jones, like many boys who grew up in the 1950s, was riveted by the sight of what he knew as an adult to be "radical evil." Among the photos taken and labeled by the Allied forces that Jones came across was one aerial image of Auschwitz-Birkenau that he calls "unexpected."[12] He writes: "Gazing down into the picture it is clear to see that within a few yards of the crematorium there was a formal garden whose design is easily recognizable as the cosmic plan." From this observation Jones concluded that, "because the garden was situated between the 'entrance gate' and the 'undressing room,' one has to imagine that for hundreds of thousands the unexpected garden provided their final glimpse of the world." In his research Jones discovered that Dr. Joachim Caesar, director of the Agricultural Division of Auschwitz, drafted certain prisoners to serve on the *Landwirtschaftskommando*, or "landscape squad." These relative few were saved from certain death but condemned to a psychological purgatory in which they were forced to "create a relative goodness out of radical evil."

The garden Jones derived from this image began as a series of models and has evolved into actual gardens based on the cosmic plan in Curitiba, Brazil, and Borås, Sweden (he has also created paradise gardens in Rethymnon, Crete, and Berlin). Jones identifies with the prisoner-landscapist of the *Pflanzenzucht*—the special plant-cultivation section of the Agricultural Division that built the cosmic garden—who becomes an artist in a Faustian position. In the case of the Auschwitz gardener, art was the vehicle for survival. But, to a degree, all artists who choose to address the unspeakable walk a thin line between the facts and their aestheticization. While not motivated by survival, Jones confronts horror and finds within it a moment of ambiguity, in the act of creating the garden. The cosmic garden at Auschwitz-Birkenau is conceivably one of the most spiritually laden, if all-but-forgotten,

Queens Museum of Art
Down the Garden Path

Chapter 1
Hell: The Memorial

(opposite page, from top)
Two archival views of
Langemarckplatz and detail of
fallen WWI soldiers' names,
Nordhorn, Germany
Photo of engraved flagstones:
Eva Ungar

(opposite page, bottom)
Nazi rally at Langemarckplatz,
Nordhorn, Germany, 1934

(this page)
Jenny Holzer
Black Garden, 1994
Concentric black planting with
five Bentheimer red sandstone
benches, and small white garden
Nordhorn, Germany

Photos (clockwise from top):
Karin Hessmann / Centrum,
André Sobott, Klaus Frahm

{31}

gardens in the Western world. Clearly the artifice of this Eden at the very heart of Hell, its theatricalization through the forced passage of walking by it, made the beauty of nature into a foil for prejudice and death.

There are gardens where misery is born and gardens born out of misery. Brian Tolle's Irish Hunger Memorial, commissioned in 2002 for New York City's Battery Park, uses the potato blight in mid-nineteenth-century Ireland as a point of departure for a multifaceted retelling of history in which the garden is the epicenter of economic, political, and agricultural change in Great Britain, Europe, and America.

If you could afford a paper at the time, this is what you might have read in the *Southern Reporter* from Cork on February 8, 1846: "The duty of publishing reports of the inquests held on persons who have 'died by starvation' has now become so frequent, and such numbers are daily reaching us from every part of the county, that the limits of our space do not admit of their publication." And since you could afford the paper, the famine might not have affected you, until some weeks later when you read this in the *Cork Reporter* of March 20, 1846: "While parties in the state and elsewhere are squabbling among themselves as to what is to be deemed the starvation test, sickness and famine are already doing their work."[13] In news accounts, language and statistics superseded the fact that Great Britain had created a cemetery in its garden.

In Battery Park City, looking out on the Statue of Liberty and Ellis Island, Tolle designed a cantilevered quarter-acre plot to commemorate the 1846–50 Irish Potato Famine. The garden memorial is adorned with thirty-two stones representing each of Ireland's counties. The stones surround a hut, or "scalpeen," made of the leftover materials of a stone cottage. Spread among the symbolic potato furrows that give order to the grassy slope outside the hut are sixty-two varieties of plant life indigenous to the Connacht boglands of County Mayo. Buried beneath the garden (a siting with metaphoric resonance) yet reachable from street level is a library containing a layered and rich literature—a democratic selection of period and more recent perspectives from politicians and poets, citizens and friends of the greater Irish diaspora. This cross-section of thoughts, meant to change periodically, takes the subject of the memorial well beyond the particular. For instance, we might learn that there had been other famines in Ireland as well as in other countries, but the famine of 1846–50 took the lives of over one million people and depleted the population by another two through emigration. We might also learn about the exodus of land laborers and their dependents to the poor- and workhouses in cities throughout the British

Queens Museum of Art
Down the Garden Path

Chapter 1
Hell: The Memorial

(far left)
Ronald Jones
Cosmic Garden, 2000
Installation view, Hannover
Courtesy of the artist

(all other images)
Brian Tolle
Irish Hunger Memorial, 2002
New York
© Brian Tolle

Design team: 1100 Architect,
Gail Wittwer-Laird ASLA
Photos: Stan Ries, courtesy
of Hugh L. Carey, Battery Park
City Authority

{33}

isles, where overcrowding brought on epidemics of fever, cholera, and dysentery, and that people fled to England, to the Continent, and to the colonies, often dying in "coffin ships" on the way.

The potato itself is notably absent from the memorial, represented as neither picture nor statue. But this absence is certainly not because it is flora non grata in Irish history. In fact, the potato had saved many a starving family in the past and was the country's preferred vegetable because it was cheap, easy to grow, and provided more calories than other crops. But its status as most favored vegetable ruined its genetic variation. The several dozen or more varieties of potato, along with the grains, beans, and green vegetables planted in the gardens of early-nineteenth-century Ireland, yielded to the economic wonder of the "lumper" and the "cup." These potatoes were also favored by *Phytophthora infestans*, the fungus that produced the blight and wiped out the crops of 1845, 1846, and 1848. If the potato is physically absent from the memorial it is because entire populations do not expire from rotten potatoes alone. The British government's relief efforts were disastrous. Their soup kitchens could not cope with the growing numbers of the needy and, with the banking crisis in England, they shut their doors. Irish Catholics, stripped of the right to own land under British rule and evicted from their minuscule plots of less than five acres, could not afford to buy foreign grains, let alone pay rent or taxes. The repeal of the Corn Law in 1846, which allowed foreign competition and established free trade, made no difference. Pawning everything, including the tools with which they made their trade, they ate seaweed, grass, and weeds while they watched much of their country's meat, dairy products, and grains—of which, in fact, there were plenty—being carted off to England.

The memory of famine, as represented by Tolle's commemoration of Irish suffering, is a green wedge in the wealthiest corner of Manhattan, where millions upon millions of stock shares are traded hourly in a global marketplace. "Remember the neediest," goes the slogan of a familiar New York City holiday fund drive. Let's hope we do, or famines will continue to feed revolutions.

Reversible Destiny

For over three decades, Shusaku Arakawa and Madeline Gins have developed their concept of "reversible destiny." This comprehensive proposal, which takes the form of a set of written instructions as well as two- and three-dimensional models and actual architecture, invites open minds to explore ways to "reorder the body radically so that it might elude mortality"[14] and represents an ongoing investigation that includes practical and aesthetic procedures for reinventing our built environment and ourselves.

The artists begin with the idea that we do not understand what we are, that most people live in resignation, or worse, in a kind of desperation and socialized "defeatist position" in which death is thought to be inevitable. A call for a "procedural constructing of the world" through architecture is a call for financial, physical, spiritual, and communal investment in resolving basic existential questions that have held the human species in a "crisis ethics." With "architecture [as] the greatest tool available to our species ['an organism-person'] needs to be defined together with that within which it moves [and] the surroundings need to be defined together with bodies moving within them."[15]

Arakawa and Gins's actualized architectures put into motion the procedures for a reversible destiny. One of their more recent architectural projects

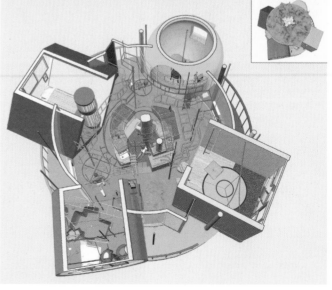

Queens Museum of Art
Down the Garden Path

Chapter 1
Hell: The Memorial

(clockwise from top)
Arakawa + Gins
*Site of Reversible Destiny—
Yoro*, 1993-95
Gifu Prefecture, Japan
Courtesy of the artists

Arakawa + Gins
*Site of Reversible Destiny—
Yoro*, 1993-95
Gifu Prefecture, Japan
Aerial view
Courtesy of the artists

Arakawa + Gins
Rendering of bathroom,
Reversible Destiny Apartment,
2002-2005
Computer-generated image
Courtesy of the artists

Arakawa + Gins
Rendering of *Reversible Destiny
Apartment*, 2002-2005
Computer-generated image
Courtesy of the artists

{35}

is a large garden, *Site of Reversible Destiny—Yoro*, situated in Gifu, Japan. Completed in 1995, *Site of Reversible Destiny—Yoro* extends some of the conceptual vocabulary found in the 1992–94 project *Ubiquitous Site▪Nagi's Ryoanji▪Architectural Body*;[16] in both, the visitor is invited to participate in a series of physical and perceptual exercises that demand a willingness to alter preconceived notions about movement in space. *Yoro* includes a main pavilion, *Critical Resemblance House*, and many smaller pavilions inside a very large grassy basin called the *Elliptical Field*. Within the *Elliptical Field* is a network of overlapping paths that lead to and from the pavilions, which are themselves architectural offshoots of aspects of the main pavilion. Superimposed on the surface of the basin are variously sized maps of Japan. Within the contours of the largest grows an array of twenty-four species of medicinal herbs, which naturally flower at different times in the season. The healing presence of nature is also found in Arakawa and Gins's yet-to-be-realized proposal for a *Museum of Living Bodies*, 2005, a retirement community of clustered living units with garden roofs.

If we take the garden memorial as a remembrance of the past and a counsel for the future, then the work of Arakawa and Gins is an *antimemorial*, a total rejection of death in which architecture and nature can only be at the service of a new concept for living. Their ideas take history out of itself and begin with a *tabula rasa*, a place where all have been but that all have forgotten. At that zero point, new phenomenal and cognitive experiences encourage a sense of potential and perhaps promote the concept of immortality.

NOTES

[1] Joachim Wolschke-Bulmahn, *The Nationalization of Nature and the Neutralization of the German Nation: "Teutonic" Trends in Early Twentieth-Century Landscape Design*, Nature and Ideology: Natural Garden Design in the Twentieth Century series, vol. 18, (Washington, DC: Dumbarton Oaks Research Library and Collection, 1997).

[2] Simon Schama, *Landscape and Memory* (New York: Vintage Books, 1995), 118.

[3] Gaius Cornelius Tacitus, ca. 54–117 AD, Roman historian; at the end of the first century AD he wrote *Germania*, a historical account of the nomadic Teutonic tribes.

[4] I have chosen to use the translation of this phrase as accepted by Erwin Panofsky and as it appears in the monograph on Ian Hamilton Finlay by Ives Abrioux. For a discussion of the interpretation of this phrase in relation to Finlay's work, see Abrioux, *Ian Hamilton Finlay: A Visual Primer*, 2nd edition (London: Reaktion Books, 1992), 241–44.

[5] Ibid., 241.

[6] Ibid., 247.

[7] Ian Hamilton Finlay, "Unconnected Sentences on Gardening," in ibid., 40.

[8] Biographical Notes, in ibid., 1.

[9] Justin Hoffmann, *Jenny Holzer: Black Garden* (Nordhorn, Germany: Städtische Galerie, 1994), 60.

[10] These and subsequent quotations about Langemarck and Nordhorn ibid., 62.

[11] The artist's father was assigned to a US Air Force unit in charge of taking aerial photographs of concentration camps used to determine bombing targets.

[12] This account and quotations from Ronald Jones, *Caesar's Cosmic Garden* (Curitiba, Brazil: Fundacão Cultural de Curitiba, 1995).

[13] Facts on the Irish Famine from period journals were taken from www.people.virgina.edu.

[14] All quotes and my description of the artists' work are entirely derived from Madeline Gins and Arakawa, *Architectural Body* (Tuscaloosa, AL, and London: University of Alabama Press, 2002); this quote page xvii.

[15] Ibid., xx.

[16] See in these pages Chapter 1, "Play: Public Gardens."

THINK-TANK RETIREMENT COMMUNITY (WISDOM CIRCLE OF ELDERS)

ZOETIC REGENE

THE SYMBOLIZING CREATURE'S LIFESPAN-INCREASING PRACTICE AREA

FOCUSING/IMAGING PARTNERSHIP

The endpoints of the labyrinth give rise to an arcade that in its turn generates the building's main arcade to which the rotations of the basic-generative units attach.

Incised into the courtyard's hilly terrain: **A LABYRINTH**

LABORATORY LUNCHEONETTE Customers will receive print-outs detailing chemical composition and nutritional benefits of menu items.

GIFT SHOP

BY PLAYING OFF OF AND JOINING FORCES WITH A SEQUENCE OF CALIBRATED ARCHITECTURAL VOLUMES, LIVING BODIES WILL COME TO KNOW ALL THAT THEY CAN BE.

ARAKAWA + GINS

Queens Museum of Art
Down the Garden Path

Chapter 1
Hell: The Memorial

Arakawa + Gins
Museum of Living Bodies, 2005
Computer-generated image
Courtesy of the artists

{37}

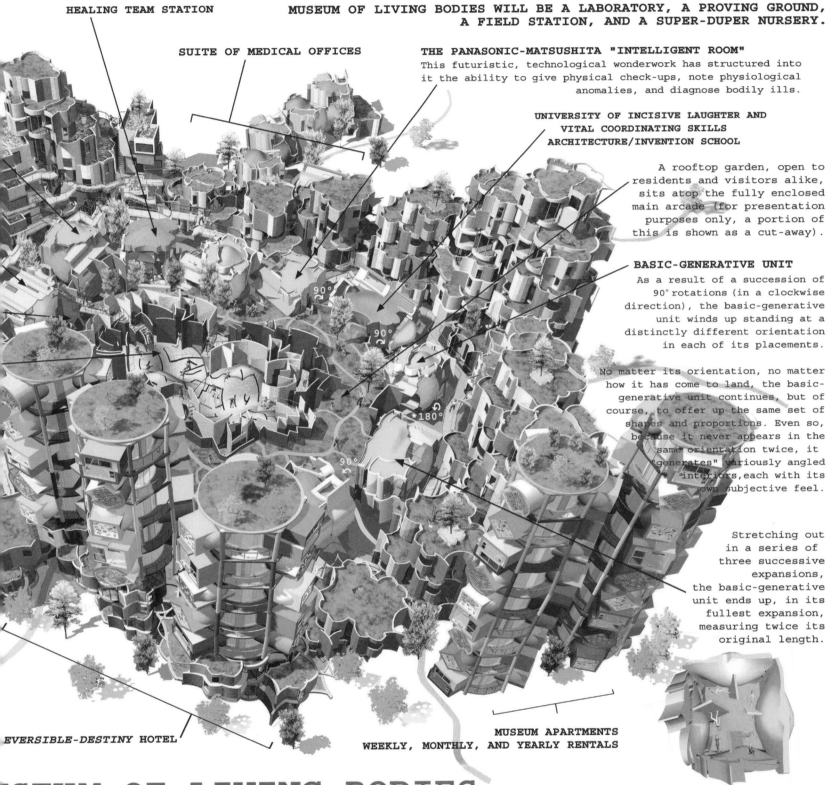

HEALING TEAM STATION

MUSEUM OF LIVING BODIES WILL BE A LABORATORY, A PROVING GROUND, A FIELD STATION, AND A SUPER-DUPER NURSERY.

SUITE OF MEDICAL OFFICES

THE PANASONIC-MATSUSHITA "INTELLIGENT ROOM"
This futuristic, technological wonderwork has structured into it the ability to give physical check-ups, note physiological anomalies, and diagnose bodily ills.

UNIVERSITY OF INCISIVE LAUGHTER AND VITAL COORDINATING SKILLS ARCHITECTURE/INVENTION SCHOOL

A rooftop garden, open to residents and visitors alike, sits atop the fully enclosed main arcade (for presentation purposes only, a portion of this is shown as a cut-away).

BASIC-GENERATIVE UNIT
As a result of a succession of 90° rotations (in a clockwise direction), the basic-generative unit winds up standing at a distinctly different orientation in each of its placements.

No matter its orientation, no matter how it has come to land, the basic-generative unit continues, but of course, to offer up the same set of shapes and proportions. Even so, because it never appears in the same orientation twice, it "generates" variously angled interiors, each with its own subjective feel.

Stretching out in a series of three successive expansions, the basic-generative unit ends up, in its fullest expansion, measuring twice its original length.

EVERSIBLE-DESTINY HOTEL

MUSEUM APARTMENTS
WEEKLY, MONTHLY, AND YEARLY RENTALS

JSEUM OF LIVING BODIES

BASIC-GENERATIVE UNIT/2003

Play: Public and Private Gardens

Public Gardens

Play happens in garden settings both public and private. The role of leisure as it developed through images that conveyed the message of movement, of progress and the future, contrasts starkly with the essentially medieval garden ideal of enclosure, isolation, and meditation—an interior search away from the energetic, often aggressive challenges of the town or city. The dialogue between outside and inside, between space and place, between the horizontality of the landscape and the verticality of the cloister, is at the crux of the definitions of public and private gardens.

How such space is framed and articulated by an artist can, as Isamu Noguchi pointed out, "quicken our senses, make them acute or deepen our perceptions to the extent where we forget time."[1] At a high point in his career, Noguchi became disillusioned with the New York art world. He thought sculpture had become decor for the wealthy and that a "new relationship between the sculptor and society should be evolved"; an opportunity to influence that dynamic was found in leisure spaces, especially in a country like the United States, which had exchanged spiritual sustenance for commercialism. In 1949 Noguchi received a research travel fellowship from the Bollingen Foundation "to study the physical environment of leisure," with a particular interest in providing children with less-inhibited recreation and play. Noguchi believed that such study would "be of great importance as a wedge in a new evaluation of living."

Noguchi left New York to travel through Europe to Greece, Egypt, India, Sri Lanka, Indonesia, Cambodia, Thailand, and Japan. He would return to the latter, his father's home country, several times as he extended his study over seven years, well beyond the fellowship's original thirty-six-month period. With a cross-cultural approach, he set out to not only understand the "relationship between the emotional

stability of a community and its physical appearance" but to affect that appearance by placing art in leisure environments. "It is an aesthetic matter," Noguchi wrote, "and as such, able to change the very kind and quality of leisure." To this end he developed prototypes for playground typologies, inspired by the prehistoric Great Serpent Mound in Adams County, Ohio, and the Jantar Mantar, an astronomical instrument built ca. 1734 by the Maharajah Sawai Jai Singh II in Jaipur, India. With few exceptions, Noguchi's progressive designs for playgrounds remained unrealized; when proposed to Robert Moses at the New York City Department of Parks and Recreation, they were rejected as too dangerous.[2] Despite these setbacks, Noguchi reworked his playful design concepts into later projects such as the garden for the Reader's Digest Building, Tokyo (1951); the UNESCO gardens in Paris (1956-58); and the Sunken Garden at Chase Manhattan Bank Plaza, New York (1961-64), all of which vary the spatial relations between their fountains and the plantings, stones or sculptural groups, never succumbing to static symmetrical arrangements.

Known primarily as a pioneer of contemporary graphic design and an important architect of the Bauhaus era, Herbert Bayer emigrated to the United States in 1938. He is often credited as being the first artist to create an "earthwork," the *Grass Mound,* in 1955. While Noguchi predated him by twenty-two years with his 1933 drawing and model for the unrealized *Monument to the Plow,*[3] Bayer's *Grass Mound* was realized as a "landscape feature embellishing a garden"[4] at the Aspen Art Institute in Colorado, and Bayer later used it as the generator for both his Anderson Park (1973-74) in Aspen and Mill Creek Canyon Earthwork (1979-82) in Kent, Washington. Commissioned by the Kings County Arts Commission and Parks and Recreation Department, Mill Creek was designed to resolve a severe problem with urban stormwater runoff and resultant soil erosion. The beauty of the work is that it does exactly that while also serving the recreational needs of the public. Bayer's idea of integrating the ecological with the aesthetic in a people's park is at the core of Bauhaus philosophy. What is unusual in the design of the park, and what we see beginning to operate in the *Grass Mound,* is the relationship of geometric forms to the landscape and how they have a role beyond the purely iconographic.

Artists Madeline Gins and Shusaku Arakawa have approached the big questions of life with great deliberation. They have created a philosophy and a practice predicated on the belief that real social reform is possible through art. While this idealism is shared by increasingly few, Gins and Arakawa remain radical about the terms and conditions in which this should occur and have over the years stepped up their efforts towards new kinds of environments that intend a "reversible destiny."

In their seminal work *Ubiquitous Site ▪ Nagi's Ryoanji ▪ Architectural Body,* 1992-94, the artists created a series of "landing sites" and containers in which the body finds its orientation by becoming one with the architectural surround. *Ubiquitous Site* was commissioned by and is set on the grounds of the Museum of Contemporary Art at Nagi, Japan, and, as its title suggests, Gins and Arakawa have appropriated aspects of Ryoanji, one of the world's oldest extant gardens (ca. 1490), located in Kyoto. By citing Ryoanji, the artists evoke a national symbol that stirs up for the Japanese strong feelings for the culture of their country, for home, for the sanctity of life, all in their purest forms. But the artists quickly cut short the viewer's reverie. Instantaneous recognition is intercepted by a progression of perceptual betrayals in the

Queens Museum of Art
Down the Garden Path

Chapter 1
Play: Public and
Private Gardens

(center, right center,
and bottom center)
Isamu Noguchi
Studies of rocks and waves for
Sunken Garden for Chase
Manhattan Bank Plaza, New York,
ca. 1960
Pen on paper, 22 x 18 inches each

Courtesy of the Noguchi
Museum, New York

(bottom right)
Isamu Noguchi
Study of rocks and waves
for Sunken Garden for
Chase Manhattan Bank Plaza,
New York, ca. 1960

Gelatin-silver print,
34½ x 32½ inches
Courtesy of the Noguchi
Museum, New York

(bottom left)
Isamu Noguchi
Sunken Garden for Beinecke
Rare Book and Manuscript

Library, 1960–64
Yale University, New Haven, CT
Photo: Shigeo Anzai

All Noguchi images © 2005 The
Isamu Noguchi Foundation and
Garden Museum, New York/Artists
Rights Society (ARS), New York

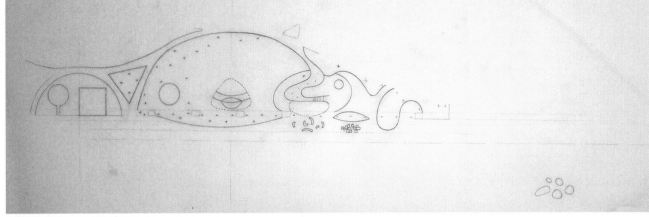

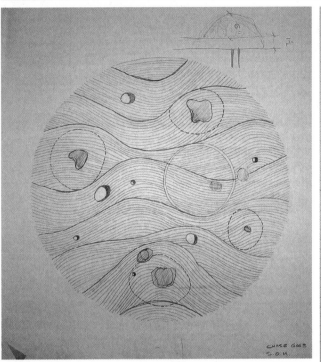

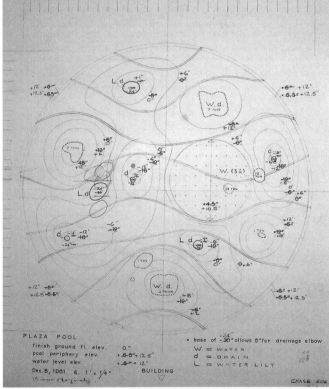

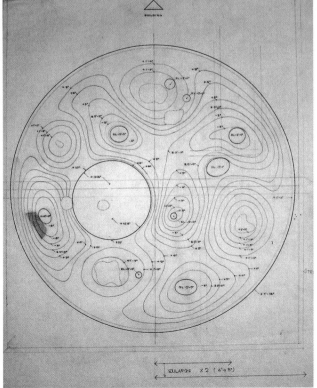

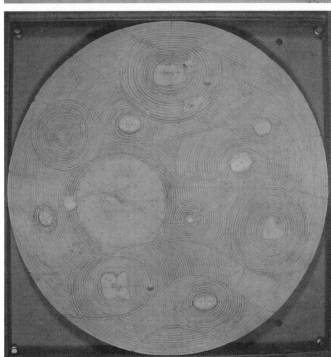

(clockwise from top left)
Herbert Bayer
Anderson Park, 1973–74
Aspen, CO
Photo: Courtesy Herbert Bayer
Collection and Archive, Denver
Art Museum, 1987.528

Herbert Bayer
Grass Mound, 1955
Aspen Art Institute, CO
Photo: Courtesy Herbert Bayer
Collection and Archive, Denver
Art Museum, 1986.1967

Herbert Bayer
*Earthworks, Mill Creek Canyon,
Kent*, 1982
Printed poster
Gift of the Estate of Herbert
Bayer, Herbert Bayer Collection
and Archive, Denver Art Museum,
b.16.2 c1

Herbert Bayer
Study for *Positive-Negative
Grass Sculpture*, 1954
Herbert Bayer Collection and
Archive, Denver Art Museum,
Gift of Joella Bayer, de.3.78

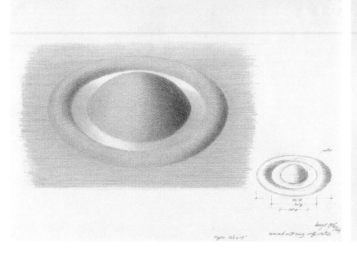

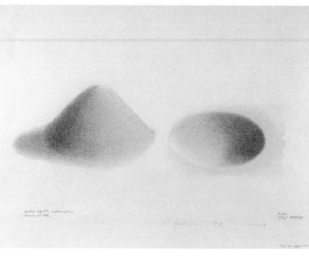

Herbert Bayer
Studies for *Grass Spiral
Mounds*, 1969
Herbert Bayer Collection and
Archive, Denver Art Museum,
Gift of Joella Bayer, de.3.82

Herbert Bayer
Study for *Positive-Negative
Earth Sculpture (mound and
hole)*, 1954/1978
Herbert Bayer Collection and
Archive, Denver Art Museum,
Gift of Joella Bayer, de.3.83

Herbert Bayer
Study for *Mound with Ring
of Water*, 1956
Herbert Bayer Collection and
Archive, Denver Art Museum,
Gift of Joella Bayer, de.3.89

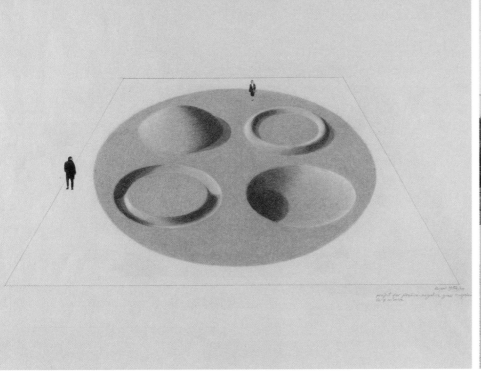

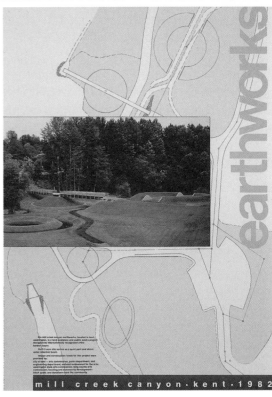

strange architectural landing sites, tactile spaces that reorient the body and prompt a reconceptualization of its function in its environment. One might conceive of the experience as a return to a prenatal sensorium.

The "Heart" section of *Ubiquitous Site* is a thirty-foot-diameter tube into which the viewer enters to experience a manipulated Ryoanji that doubles that garden's content: scholar's stones, gravel patterns, viewing benches, and seesaws. This symmetrical space negates both one-point perspective and two as well as three dimensions in favor of a different, zero-gravitational dimension. Walking through this cylinder, nothing is taken for granted—all bodily actions are to be reconsidered. The "Heart" bears some relation to the concept of *ostriani*, the perceptual estrangement described by Russian linguist Mikhail Bakhtin and visualized in the photographs of Alexander Rodchenko. More important, it proposes a radically new architectural language and set of procedures toward establishing better living through better space. Perhaps *Ubiquitous Site* is not a place for leisure as we know it today, or perhaps the language for what it is or does has not yet been invented. The phenomenological experience is extreme, akin to Haruki Murakami's descriptions of slipping into the unknown of the well in his 1997 novel *The Wind-Up Bird Chronicle*.

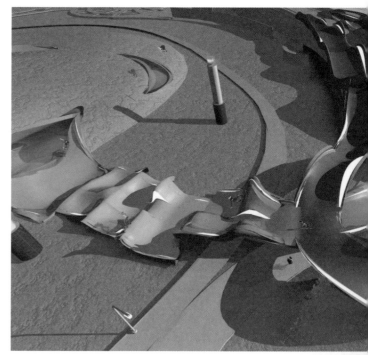

Equally structurally ambitious and provocative is the work of Vito Acconci, whose dynamic architectural and landscape projects to some degree resemble those of Roberto Burle Marx. For example, Acconci's fabulous beachfront park in San Juan, Puerto Rico, *A Skate Park That Glides the Land & Drops into the Sea* (2004), with its roller-coaster boardwalk for skateboarding, has affinities with Burle Marx's theatrical composition of palms and wave forms at Copacabana Beach in Rio de Janeiro (1970); and Acconci's earlier vertical garden, *Park Up a Building* in Santiago de Campostela (1996), hints, if distantly, at Burle Marx's wonderful modernist vertical garden for Safra Bank in São Paulo (1982). Where Acconci carries things further is in his focus on language and its manifestation as movement; he entwines the language of public gardens and icons of popular recreation with performance. In San Juan, the lines of his design move up and down, out and over the beachfront like arabesques, to elongate the concourse of play; in Santiago de Campostela, miniterraces break up sequential elevations in an almost mechanistic, stop-action march.

A performer himself, Acconci's understanding of space is through physical movement in it. He therefore creates spaces where the public can perform outdoors. In his designs, the garden/landscape functions as a reverberation and an extension of the body's movement and leads the body into spatial pockets that encourage encounters and events. Alternatively, in his *Garden Born from Gardens*, 1993, a concept for the MetroTech Center in Brooklyn (which extends the idea of Gordon Matta-Clark's 1972 *Rosebush*), nature is both the material and the message, an industrial labyrinth perhaps inspired by the intricacy of the Vedic gardens of the Alhambra in Granada, Spain.

Among the younger artists who have practiced landscape or garden interventions, a key figure is Paula Hayes. Hayes debuted at the sadly short-lived New York gallery AC Project Room in 1997 with funky installations of plants in cement containers shelved on wood scaffolding. In addition to her work as an artist, she makes minigardens that are set in soft, organically shaped cast-silicone containers, or else strapped like papooses—plantpacks—to one's body to promote longevity and kinship with nature. Now she is working with terrariums, Lilliputian green worlds in fabulously shaped bubbles of

Queens Museum of Art
Down the Garden Path

Chapter 1
Play: Public and
Private Gardens

(top left)
Acconci Studio (Vito Acconci,
Darío Núñez, Sehzat Oner,
Jeremy Linzee, Peter Dorsey,
J. Gabriel Lloyd, Sarina Basta)
*A Skate Park That Glides the
Land & Drops into the Sea*, 2004
San Juan, Puerto Rico

(bottom left)
Acconci Studio (Luis Vera,
Jenny Schrider, Charles Doherty)
Park Up a Building, 1996
Aluminum, grating, trees,
tree-bags, and fluorescent lights
Centro Gallego de Arte
Contemporanea,

Santiago de Campostela
Courtesy of the artist

(top right)
Roberto Burle Marx
Wall garden and sidewalk, 1982
Safra Bank, São Paulo
Courtesy of Burle Marx & Cia. Ltda.
Photo: Haruyoshi Ono

(bottom right)
Aerial view of Copacabana
Beach, Rio de Janeiro, showing
promenades by Roberto Burle
Marx (completed 1970)
Courtesy of Burle Marx & Cia. Ltda.
Photo: Haruyoshi Ono

blown glass. Hayes's talent and acclaim have launched her into a world of more stylish clients and more substantial gardens. Without losing her edge (Hayes's garden proposal for the outdoor component of "Down the Garden Path," which incorporated graffiti into a nature/culture nook of urban detritus, was categorically rejected by an antigraffitist on the jury), she continues to combine brash plastic materials with pure horticulture in city settings, albeit in more prominent sites. Hayes's associations with older artists have been bold and transforming. Consciously or unconsciously, her curvilinear shapes and her guerrilla approach to the garden owes much to Acconci. But the tension created by juxtaposing lush nature with an urban public context is very much in keeping with the Burle Marx aesthetic of mixing bright, patterned mosaics with explosions of indigenous plant life.

The Kraus Campo (2004), Mel Bochner's first garden (made in collaboration with landscape architect Michael Van Valkenburgh), is named after its patrons, Jill and Peter Kraus. The garden is partially surrounded by the College of Fine Arts and the Tepper School of Business at Pittsburgh's Carnegie Mellon University, the artist's alma mater. While the garden is public, it is also elevated and partially enclosed, so that people have to go there deliberately rather than wander through it. Therefore it functions not as a transitional space between classes but as a place to eat, relax, think, and discuss.

While curves are sadly more a novelty than a necessity in architecture, we take them for granted in landscape design. In the Kraus Campo, however, the French curve announces itself emphatically as the iconographic apex of the garden, the point at which all paths lead in and out. The surface of the French curve is a raised bed made up of porcelain tiles printed with the numbers 0 to 9. These numbers, which are rotated in a random pattern, recall ancient Indian and Arabic mathematical systems that both have spiritual uses and provide the basic principles of architecture and physics. These are the very foundations on which the French curve was created—something to think about while you are sitting on it eating lunch.

The second significant element in the garden is a discrete work by Bochner. *You Can Call It That If You Like*, 2004, a set of porcelain tiles mounted on the wall of the business school, quotes a text by Ludwig Wittgenstein, whose contributions on language and its relation to the world greatly influenced Bochner's generation. The text, taken from Wittgenstein's writings on culture,[5] is written in reverse, an encryption that playfully challenges the uninitiated:

> ".IN WALK THEY DIRECTION THE CHANGED HAVE PEOPLE THAT THAN MORE NO SAID HAVE YOU THAT MIND YOUR IN CLEAR BE SHOULD YOU THEN BUT :LIKE YOU IF THAT IT CALL CAN YOU COURSE OF .DAY ONE BACKWARDS WALKING START SHOULD MEN IF DIRECTION ITS CHANGE WOULD TIME :THIS TO COMES ENTROPY OF LAW THE AND 'TIME OF DIRECTION THE' ABOUT SAYS EDDINGTON WHAT"

If one is not immediately aware that this text is written in reverse, it reads like a rebus, with the main clue to a possible connection with the French curve being the name of British mathematician, astronomer, and physicist Arthur Eddington (1882-1944). Eddington's research in the field of astrophysics proved Einstein's theory that the path of light is bent by gravity as it passes a massive star. The Kraus Campo consists of a contiguous series of curves that lead off and back to the French curve; in other words, it plays the visual counterpart to Wittgenstein's text, which conveys the main principles of the second law of thermodynamics, that any isolated system is in a constant state of disorder, or entropy. But since most systems are interrelated,

Queens Museum of Art
Down the Garden Path

Chapter 1
Play: Public and
Private Gardens

(clockwise from right)
Paula Hayes
Plantpack, 2000
Demonstration view
Courtesy of the artist

Paula Hayes
Jill's Poet's Paper, 2003
Pencil, marker, glitter, and
glue on archival bond paper,
90 x 60 inches
Courtesy of the artist

Paula Hayes
The Ineradicable Unknown
(Proposal for "Down the Garden
Path"), 2004
Rendering, 8 x 8 inches
Courtesy of the artist

Paula Hayes
*Hand-Blown Glass Terrarium
with Living Plants*, 2004
13 x 20 x 20 inches
Courtesy of the artist

16 JAN 03

Queens Museum of Art
Down the Garden Path

Chapter 1
Play: Public and
Private Gardens

(clockwise from left)
Mel Bochner
The Campo, 2004
Laser-cut porcelain tile and
stainless steel on poured
concrete, 60 x 30 x 3 feet
Courtesy of the artist
Photo: Tim Kaulen

Mel Bochner and
Michael Van Valkenburgh
Kraus Campo, 2004
Carnegie Mellon University,
Pittsburgh
Courtesy of the artist
Photo: Heather Mull

Mel Bochner
*You Can Call It That If You
Like*, 2004
Laser-cut porcelain tile on
painted wall, 6 x 60 feet
Courtesy of the artist
Photo: Annie O'Neill

Mel Bochner
Campo Sketch, 2003
Colored pencil on paper and
digital rendering, 7 ½ x 14 inches
Courtesy of the artist

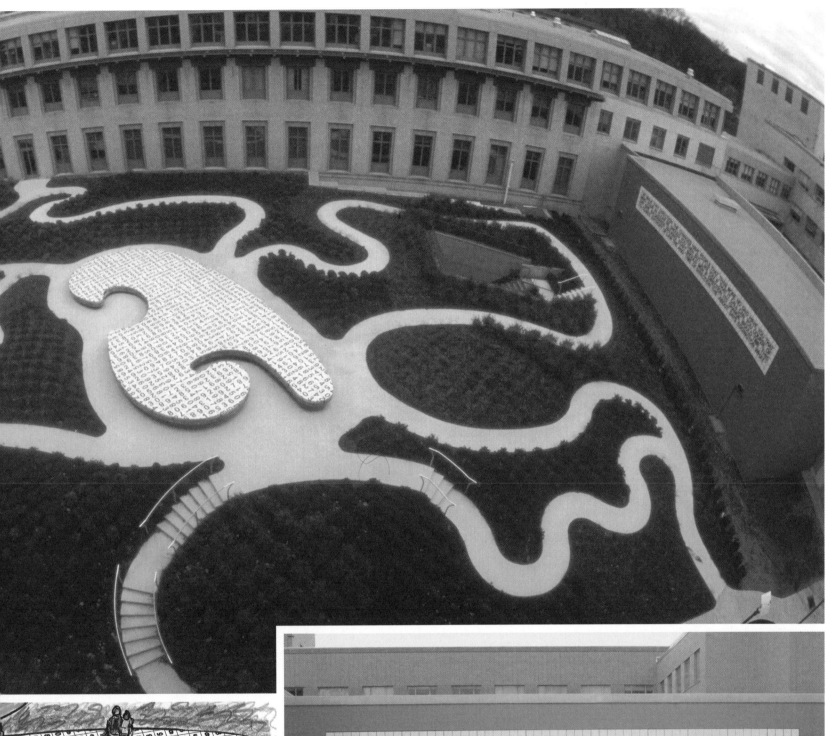

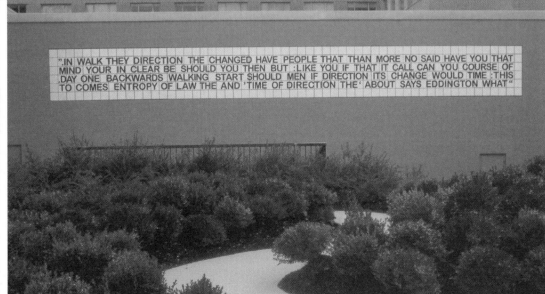

the first law of thermodynamics balances this disorder through the process of conversion: Energy is taken in one form and converted into another; order and disorder even out. The text is thus a kind of poetic formula for the design of the garden. Walk in any direction and one expends energy, but gains new vigor through the process.

Another garden that takes as its coordinates for construction basic geometry—the circle, square, triangle, and ellipse—is Lothar Baumgarten's *Theatrum Botanicum*,[6] a *hortus conclusus* (enclosed garden) inaugurated in 1994 at the Fondation Cartier in Paris. A *theatrum botanicum* is both a theater and a botanical garden, a place in which nature, in the form of an encyclopedia of native or foreign species, sets the stage for a potential event. Like Bochner's Kraus Campo, Baumgarten's garden is open to the public yet secluded from traffic, a green space that encourages discussion as a respite from the visual stimulus within. *Theatrum Botanicum* is both a place for reflection and one that reflects the relationship between medieval walled gardens and European illuminated manuscripts and tapestries. The delicate flowers depicted in these images, with their rich associations in the arts of cuisine, medicine, and jewelry making, were the key to the plantings within the actual garden. Each corner of the garden is carefully considered, with color arrangements and horticultural symbolism at play.

At certain times of day, the glazed architecture of Jean Nouvel's Fondation Cartier building, which the garden surrounds, reflects Baumgarten's grassy carpet and meticulous plantings. Nouvel's large, fenestrated entrance reveals the interior from all sides, refracting the sun's rays so intensely that all distinction between building and garden disappears. On this brilliantly mirrored surface, pockets of visibility are created by the shadows of trees, making transparent patches that penetrate through so that one can glimpse the inside. As the artist has said: "Magic is . . . when abstraction, based both on geometric and mathematic orders and on the notion of iconography, leads all involved elements through intuition to a basic spatial concept."[7] Baumgarten follows an ancient tradition in the way he derives his spatial events from the original site plans—the footprint of the actual plot and the science of given points that in turn yield abstract forms. In combination, these forms lock in a sense of universal meaning further underscored by the symbolic fountain and surrounding theater at the garden's center.

Invited to create a work for the 1998 Manifesta, a roving biennial of contemporary European art, Tobias Rehberger selected a site directly opposite architect Jean Prouvé's 1958 addition to the former nineteenth-century Casino Bourgeois, now the Pavilion de Luxembourg, that city's art center. For a long time the public had forgotten that Prouvé had built an addition, until the city wanted to destroy it. When it was recalled that a great modernist had designed what was formerly considered an eyesore, the city changed its mind.

Reconsidering Luxembourg's appreciation and knowledge of modernist architecture, Rehberger created a temporary garden, *Within view of seeing (perspectives and the Prouvé)*, on a paved terrace across the street from the pavilion. Normally the public would lean over the balustrade of the terrace to see the view of the valley with the city and the park below, but Rehberger reversed the view and placed the bench facing his garden and the Prouvé. The garden, planted in overlapping, variously rectangular raised beds of cabbage, strawberries, and herbs mixed in with marigolds, petunias, and red-leafed plants, formed a brilliant "color field painting" from the building's second floor and recalled aerial views of agriculture, or the façade of the

Queens Museum of Art
Down the Garden Path

Chapter 1
Play: Public and
Private Gardens

Lothar Baumgarten
Theatrum Botanicum, 1993-94
Fondation Cartier pour l'Art
Contemporain, Paris
Garden details and sunken
fountain

© 2005 Artists Rights
Society (ARS), New York/
VG Bild-Kunst, Bonn

{51}

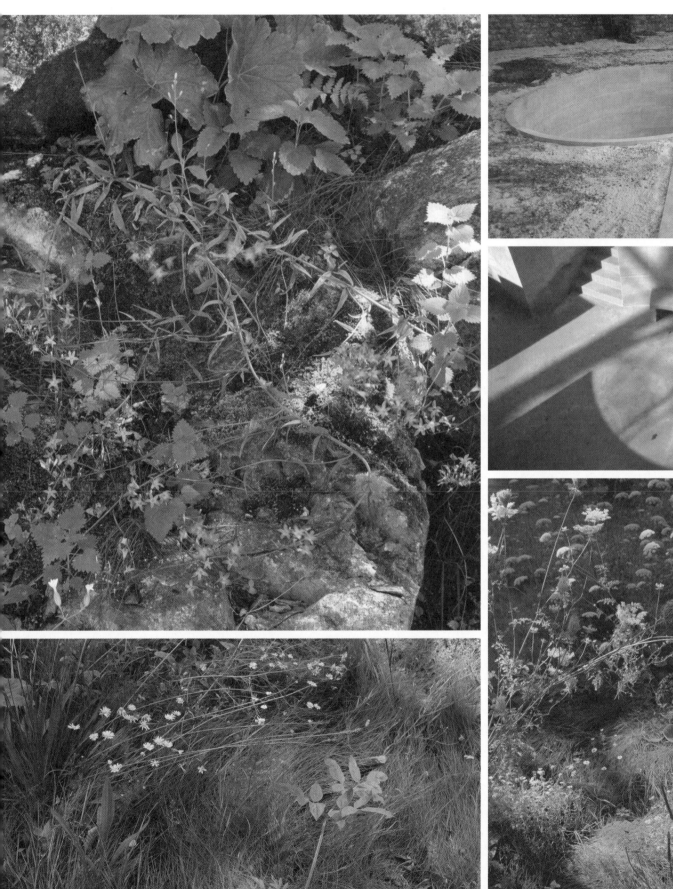

Queens Museum of Art
Down the Garden Path

Chapter 1
Play: Public and
Private Gardens

Tobias Rehberger
*Within view of seeing (perspectives
and the Prouvé),* 1998
Installation views, Manifesta II,
Pavilion de Luxembourg, 1998
Courtesy of the artist

Prouvé addition itself. This geometrically configured flower and vegetable carpet is Rehberger's homage to the pragmatic/aesthetic dialectic operating in Prouvé's modernist designs, an infatuation Rehberger has carried throughout his own work.

Among the artists who have made the most significant contributions to the relationship between gardens and architecture is Dan Graham, with his glass pavilions begun in the late 1970s. In the oft-cited article "Corporate Arcadias,"[8] Graham and Robin Hurst track the evolution of public gardens from their origins in the eighteenth-century European suburban cemetery to the urban commercial atrium, an effort to woo back businesses and consumers who began to exit city centers in the late 1960s. These glass "tents," which recall winter gardens and conservatories, have helped inspire Graham's own glass surrounds, which are frequently sited in parks and on private lawns, or in museum collections such as that of the Westfälisches Landesmuseum für Kunst und Kulturgeschichte in Münster. They are contemporary follies with curiously translucent and yet reflective surfaces, capturing the green landscape outside and—sometimes with revolving or sliding doors—trapping the viewer within, playing with our perception as we lose or gain perspectives amid the ever-shifting optical surfaces.

Jan Vercruysse's *Labyrinth & Pleasure Gardens*, two portfolios of lithographs made in 1994–95 and 2002, critique the failure of public art in parks and gardens. His rejoinder to the alienation that results from most art in public spaces is to propose the most beautiful designs possible. These plans, not yet realized, make no separation between what is a garden and what is art: The two are one and the same. The lines of Vercruysse's designs are like ciphers, seemingly dispassionate and therefore reserved. At the bottom of his plans the artist provides a key or nomenclature for recognizing the forms and their function, an indication of the technical precision with which he approaches the gardens. The entirety is a mental game, demanding in its invitation to decode, rewarding through the process of revelation. Vercruysse's designs are theoretical proposals—cerebral, iconic, and pure. A rigorous simplicity lies behind the artist's *sense du jeu*: an entrance that intrigues, a path that leads you on, an illusion that humors the spirit, a symbol that piques one's curiosity.

Private Gardens

Like the first works of art, the first pleasure gardens were sacred and private. Rulers like Nebuchadnezzar II and Louis XIV, who sought power by aligning themselves with God or posing as godly themselves, built gardens from Babylon to Versailles to signify their godliness. For millennia only the wealthy had private gardens: As items of conspicuous luxury, they had to be extraordinary and thus took huge resources to maintain. Sheer acreage in front mirrored awe-inspiring displays in back—not only of wealth and territorial possession, but of the ingenuity, knowledge, and taste of the owner and his ability to harness horticulture. Beginning with the Renaissance, the private garden was designed for amusement: a gigantic game board for battle reenactments, an arena for social games or a field for sensual experience, a trysting place, *un jardin d'amour*. The garden as status symbol was replicated and adapted to fit the wallets and whims of clients.

Queens Museum of Art
Down the Garden Path

Chapter 1
Play: Public and
Private Gardens

(right)
Dan Graham
Two-Way Mirror and Hedge, 1996
Installation view, Walker Art
Center, Minneapolis, MN
Collection Walker Art Center,
Minneapolis, MN

(left center)
Dan Graham
*Private "Public" Space: The
Corporate Atrium Garden*, 1987
One of six photomontages:
black-and-white and color photo-
graphs and photographically

reproduced texts mounted
on cardboard, 40 x 31 inches
© Generali Foundation
Collection, Vienna

(bottom left)
Dan Graham
Bridge/Pergola, 1988
Installation view, Clisson, France
Courtesy of the artist

LABYRINTH & PLEASURE GARDEN   n°6, 1994

LABYRINTH & PLEASURE GARDEN   n°9, 1995 *(für S.)*

LABYRINTH

LABYRINTH & PLEASURE GARDEN   n°17, 1998

LABYRINTH & PLEASURE GARDEN   n°19, 1998

LABYRINT

URE GARDEN   n° 12, 1995

LABYRINTH & PLEASURE GARDEN   n°16, 1997

URE GARDEN   n° 21, 2000

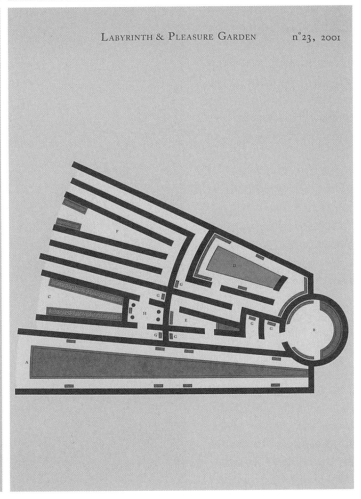

LABYRINTH & PLEASURE GARDEN   n°23, 2001

(nos. 9 and 12)
Jan Vercruysse
Labyrinth & Pleasure Gardens
(details), 1994–95
Two of eight lithographs
in cloth-bound portfolio,
26 x 19 ½ inches
Courtesy Brooke Alexander

(all others)
Jan Vercruysse
Labyrinth & Pleasure Gardens
(details), 2002
Six of thirteen lithographs
in cloth-bound portfolio,
26 x 19 ½ inches
Courtesy Brooke Alexander

(top row)
*Labyrinth & Pleasure Garden
no. 6*, 1994
"A circular garden divided into
ten gardens, with a cascading
basin [A]; two oval basins with
circular fountains [B]; two elliptical basins [C]; three small stone
benches in front of a basin with
goldfish and small fountains [D];
a three-part high-walled basin
with fountains and stone benches
[E]; two half-circular basins and
a stone bench [F]; two high-walled
curved basins with lower stone
benches [G]; a stone-bordered
basin with two stone-bordered
lawns at a deeper level [H]; a
borderless basin in a white and
blue mosaic floor and a long
dark grey stone bench [I]; two
elliptical basins confined in
two not-elliptical basins [J]; a
circular blue stone pavement
with a not completely closed
circular stone bench [L]; and a
few small stone benches [K]."

*Labyrinth & Pleasure Garden
no. 9*, 1995
"A rillet with a paved border [A]; a
pond with a terracotta surround
[B], in a garden with a field of tall
grasses [C]."

*Labyrinth & Pleasure Garden
no. 12*, 1995
"A walking path around a garden
[A]; a long lane diving two lawns
with no flowers at all [B]; a basin
with a fountain in an elliptical
court [C]; a reading garden with a
stone bench and a small basin
with a fountain [D]; a garden with
two red rose beds [E]; a reading
and conversation garden with a
stone bench and a small basin
with a fountain [F]; a garden with
two small stone benches and
a basin with goldfish and a fountain [G]; and a conversation
garden with two stone benches
and a basin with goldfish and a
fountain [H]."

*Labyrinth & Pleasure Garden
no. 16*, 1997
"A garden with a black swan lake
and eleven small stone benches
[A]; a circular garden with a pond
and a fountain and one long circular stone bench [B]; a garden
for triangular conversations [C];

a small circular garden with an
eye-shaped basin and a fountain
[D]; and a small stone bench at
the end of a walk [E]."

(bottom row)
*Labyrinth & Pleasure Garden
no. 17*, 1998
"A pavement and two benches
made of smoothed yellow ochre
flagstone [A]; a triangular basin
bordered with smoothed yellow
ochre flagstone and a small
fountain [B]; a circular garden
with three benches made of
smoothed yellow ochre flagstone
for radial conversations [C]; a
slightly elevated platform and
a bench for no conversation at
all, made of smoothed yellow
ochre flagstone, and a borderless basin with fast-running
water [D]; and an L-shaped
bench made of smoothed yellow ochre flagstone [E]."

*Labyrinth & Pleasure Garden
no. 19*, 1998
"A garden with a small curved
red marble bench in front of a
pond and a black granite and a
red granite bench [A]; a garden
with a pond and two black granite benches [B]; and in a walk two
small red granite benches and
one small black granite bench
[C]; and a curved stone bench at
the end of that walk [D]; and a
garden with a pond surrounding
an exedra with a basin and a
fountain bordered with red granite and two small red granite
benches and two large black
granite benches [E]."

*Labyrinth & Pleasure Garden
no. 21*, 2000
"A circular basin around a garden
with a basin and a fountain in the
centre of a stone pavement and
a very long stone bench and two
shorter stone benches and four
stone benches."

*Labyrinth & Pleasure Garden
no. 23*, 2001
"A garden with a pond with fast-
running water and eight stone
benches [A]; an exedra with a
terracotta basin and fountains
and two curved stone benches
[B]; a garden with two elevated
stone basins for seasonal flowers and imperatively in autumn
tall-growing dahlias with semi-
cactus and cactus flower heads
[C]; a garden with a red rose bed
and stone benches [D]; a small
garden with a small basin and
few goldfish and a stone bench
[E]; a garden with two high-
walled basins with fountains [F];
some small stone benches [G];
and a monologic garden with a
small stone bench and four terracotta vases each with a short-
pruned monkey puzzle
(Araucaria araucana) [H]."

Of course, not all great private gardens are the product of patronage or privilege. The artist's garden, an imaginary place or a living studio, is a domain of endless calculation and critical adjustment disclosed to a fortunate few. The attribute that unites their disparate ways is the uncompromising passion with which their makers exercise their individualities through them.

To describe modernist artist Alfonso Ossorio's drive to amass the most important collection of conifers in the United States—if not the world—as "obsessive" might be too modest a characterization. Over twenty years on sixty acres of land in South Hampton, New York, known as the Creeks, he not only collected a seemingly infinite number of species and variants of conifer but constantly displaced and rearranged the trees to avoid their outshining one another within his carefully balanced composition. But it was not enough to stop there: "Ossorio kept voluminous files and photographic records of every tree in his collection, including Latin names, sources and costs, location of each specimen on the property, fertilizer schedules, and even extensive documentation of storm damage and clean-ups."[9] The artist's archive, which includes 15,000 books—many of which, as one would imagine, pertain to gardens and landscape design and theory—speaks to his organizational bent. Ossorio's artistic side, however, was expressed in his revolutionary approach to the landscape. He practiced a kind of science fiction, grafting odd varieties of firs onto other species to develop strange, experimental hybrids he called "'monsters' of horticulture." His palette and sense of form were unadulterated, bold, beyond nature.

Given Ossorio's accumulative garden aesthetic (which paralleled that of his artworks per se, thickly impastoed congregations of found natural and synthetic materials on wood panels), it is unsurprising to learn that he housed his friend Jean Dubuffet's collection of *Art Brut*, the largest in America.[10] Ossorio's emphasis on texture and fluid forms gave the conifers of the Creeks a rough immediacy, looming and wild like Dubuffet's surfaces. His outdoor sculptures, meanwhile, with their bright colors and geometric shapes, played with and against the abundant verdure of the gardenlike toys amidst a forest of unruly Christmas trees. Ossorio's sense of *horror vacui*—evidenced by the profusion of conifers married with his indefatigable decorative impulse—grants him a prominent place as an American Surrealist.

The uninhibited playfulness in Ossorio's sculptures is also evident in the found pieces that punctuate Derek Jarman's garden in Dungeness, England. There is an inescapable sense of kitsch about the filmmaker, a true enjoyment of bad taste and *je m'en foutisme* that Jarman cultivated at a young age and let run wild in his garden and films. He makes merry with the gnomes and trolls that poked up out of the suburban lawns of his childhood by substituting for them found detritus from the beaches of Dungeness. But this aspect of his garden only serves as a prelude to a developed militancy that plays out in the garden as a whole.

Jarman discovered Dungeness in 1986 while motoring around Kent looking for a landscape to film—footage that would become his film *The Garden* (1990). Taken with the extreme climate of the place, which features fierce easterlies and burning sun and salt, Jarman bought an isolated and abandoned little cottage that faced the region's nuclear-power plant. Natural accidents of driftwood placement and the indigenous plants and shrubs inspired Jarman to cultivate a garden that over the next twelve years would become a great passion in his life. Rebutting the traditional gardens

Queens Museum of Art
Down the Garden Path

Chapter 1
Play: Public and
Private Gardens

(clockwise from left)
Alfonso Ossorio
The Creeks 14, 1991
Gelatin-silver print

Alfonso Ossorio
The Creeks 15, 1991
Gelatin-silver print

Alfonso Ossorio
The Creeks 8, 1991
Gelatin-silver print

Alfonso Ossorio
The Creeks 3, 1991
Gelatin-silver print

All Ossorio photos:
Robert Giard / © Estate
of Robert Giard

that are the crowning glory of England's horticultural history, Jarman's garden is wild, unforgiving, and a demonstration of political activism in its most stoic form. In constant battle with the elements and the sinister threat of the power plant in his front yard, whose radioactivity was soaked up by the sea kale, Dungeness was Jarman's beauty sleeping with the devil.

In the early 1990s Jarman became sick with AIDS. In a 1996 book, he cites an instance in which a follower of his used the Dungeness garden as a filmic metaphor for Jarman's own illness; but, as Jarman cuttingly wrote, "AIDS was too vast a subject to 'film.' All the art failed. It was well intentioned but decorative."[11] He rejected the idea that his garden was somehow a testament to his struggle with the disease and abhorred the idea that his condition would be memorialized in art, like the AIDS Memorial Quilt in the United States. Yet he did make art until his death, and the revolutionary thrust of his films reverberates in his garden. Perhaps it is best to see Jarman's garden as an antimemorial, defying a benign contemplation of the past in a garden that is itself death-defying.

The contentious mood that lingers in the air of Dungeness is a companion to the rebelliousness one finds in Stonypath, Ian Hamilton Finlay's garden and temple, a diamond in the rough of Scotland's Pentland Hills. Stonypath, the brainchild of Finlay and his former wife Sue, was bought by the couple in 1966. Its name might have stayed Stonypath if, among other things, Finlay did not like a good fight. The place gained the additional moniker Little Sparta (referring to the war between that ancient Greek city-state and neighboring Athens) as the result of the feud that eventually ensued over the local government's enforcement of property taxes. The "temple" was designated taxable, because authorities viewed it as a barn turned into an art gallery for the display of Finlay's work. Finlay, on the other hand, claimed it as "a place apart, if you like a religious place"—indeed, a garden temple dedicated to Apollo, the god of war and music—and thus beyond the law. To commemorate winning his first "battle" on February 4, 1983, Finlay erected a monument, and Little Sparta was born on the spot, living up to its namesake in many more controversies over power and property, fighting and defeating authorities of every office at every level.[12]

Finlay has always possessed a gift for debate. It appears in his adherence to vernacular rather than cultivated modernist language, in his arguments with Scottish poet Hugh MacDiarmid,[13] and in the historicist position he takes up against the new, the *tabula rasa* of the present. All of this is evident in Finlay's neoclassical Stonypath garden, where he taps the visual potential of words and letters as icons to suggest associations whose sum total has come to stand for the project of Little Sparta: his garden, his temple, and his life's work. Finlay is a specialist on the French Revolution; it's a subject to which he devotes particular attention, extrapolating from that transformative event parallels with the contemporary world. Each element that one comes across in the garden works both with and against the transitory nature that surrounds it. Neoclassical architectural fragments such as socles, capitals, and columns and various stones are inscribed with historical references that manage to be paradoxically concrete in their assertions yet elusive and complex in meaning. The fleeting implications of the word experienced in nature warns against something bigger, of repercussions in history and of consequences in the future. Like an oracular question disguised as a statement, the work taunts the intellect while it soothes the ear. To recognize the dialectic play in the garden of Little Sparta is to navigate the minefield of the Enlightenment.

Queens Museum of Art
Down the Garden Path

Chapter 1
Play: Public and
Private Gardens

(clockwise from top left)
Derek Jarman at Prospect
Cottage, Dungeness, England,
ca. 1990
Courtesy of the Estate of
Derek Jarman

Prospect Cottage, Dungeness,
England, 1991
Courtesy of the Estate of
Derek Jarman

Pages 20-21 from Derek
Jarman, *Garden Book*, vol. 2,
March-April 1989
Artist's notebook, 8 x 8 ¼ inches
Courtesy of the Estate of
Derek Jarman

Pages 54-55 from Derek
Jarman, *Garden Book*, vol. 2,
March-April 1989
Artist's notebook, 8 x 8 ¼ inches
Courtesy of the Estate of
Derek Jarman

{61}

Finlay's lighting-bolt wit is also very visible in his works on paper. For instance, he cheers the creative, exuberant results of destruction in posters and other printed matter that announce, advocate, or admonish as seen in works such as *Laconic*, 1987, a screenprint with Ron Costley; *National Flags Series, Valhalla*, 1975, a card with Michael Harvey; and *Two Landscapes of the Sublime*, 1989, a lithographic print with Gary Hincks. It's also apparent when Finlay carves words in stone like a notice or warning; and the actual object, the post or column, can have an effect like a stake through the heart. While perhaps not all of Finlay's work communicates in revolutionary terms, it does prod the viewer to think.

Writing of John Barrel's approach to the eighteenth-century English poet John Clare (whom Finlay quotes in his *Five Benches for a Lane*, 1998) and Clare's celebration of his beloved landscape of Peterborough, Jane Brown points out that the author balances the "accepted cultural idea of the eighteenth-century 'landskip', of paintings, aristocratic parks and Augustan poetry . . . [with] Clare's technique and imagination in the real context of the poor country boy in the farming fens, who had little use for the word 'Picturesque' and could only apologize for the lack of any sublime rockiness in his home landscape: 'Swamps of wild rush-beds, and sloughs' squashy traces / Grounds of rough fallows with thistle and weed / Flats and low valleys of kingcups and daisies, Sweetest of subjects are ye for my reed'."[14]

The point is that Clare was writing simply as he saw it. This was not the picturesque landscape that was the credo *de rigueur* of his day. And so, maybe, when Finlay carves the word "picturesque" along the top post of a fence leading down the bank of Lochan Eck—one dedicated to his son—he asks us to judge for ourselves whether this view of the land is truly "picturesque" in the nineteenth-century sense of the term, or whether it is just a pond, artificially constructed, with the landscape of Lanark around it. And in so doing doesn't Finlay laugh approvingly at his own creation? The joke is one of the most successful forms of protest, one produced from the difference between what we see and what we read.

Belgian artist Thierry De Cordier shares Finlay's sense of willfulness in the garden. But where Finlay barbs, De Cordier burrows, swaddling his vulnerable sculptural productions in the stuff of nature. In De Cordier's version of the garden, a brooding, existential mood consumes his expressions about country, language, landscape, and home. To feed this inclination, the artist leads a monkish life, fiercely guarding his privacy and avoiding intrusions. But disappointed we would be if his attitude changed, for his seclusion permits happy occasions to see the fruits of his cloistering.

There is a vague sense of reticence about De Cordier's work that leads the viewer on; they are circular meditations on the simple things that surround him. On long walks through the landscape and along the seaside of his native Belgium, he concretizes the spirit of the place and his connection to it in a variety of traditional media, often accompanied by legends or personal musings conveyed in great detail on canvas and paper. Monochromatic paintings of the sea and the land approach transcendence through the earnest way De Cordier immerses himself in the subject: Adopting the form of the subject at hand is how De Cordier understands the world. The pensive view out the window to the sea, the constitutional through the fields, and the isolated writing-desk in the garden are stations in a great imaginary world that prepares De Cordier for a metaphysical transition. His landscape drawings, *Paysage troué (Traverse, no. 2)* (Perforated Landscape [Traverse, no. 2]), 1996, or *Étude d'homme dans un paysage* (Study for a Man in the Landscape), 1996-99,

Queens Museum of Art
Down the Garden Path

Chapter 1
Play: Public and
Private Gardens

(clockwise from top left)
Ian Hamilton Finlay
Picturesque, n. d.
Installation view, Little Sparta,
Dunsyre, Scotland
Courtesy of the artist
Photo: Andrew Lawson

Ian Hamilton Finlay
(with Ron Costley)
Laconic, 1987
Screenprint, 29 ⅞ x 23 inches
Courtesy of Nolan/Eckman
Gallery

Ian Hamilton Finlay
Map of Little Sparta,
Dunsyre, Scotland

Ian Hamilton Finlay
(with Bob Lewis)
Five Benches for a Lane, 1998
Teak, 16 ½ x 37 x 10 inches each
Courtesy of Nolan/Eckman
Gallery

{63}

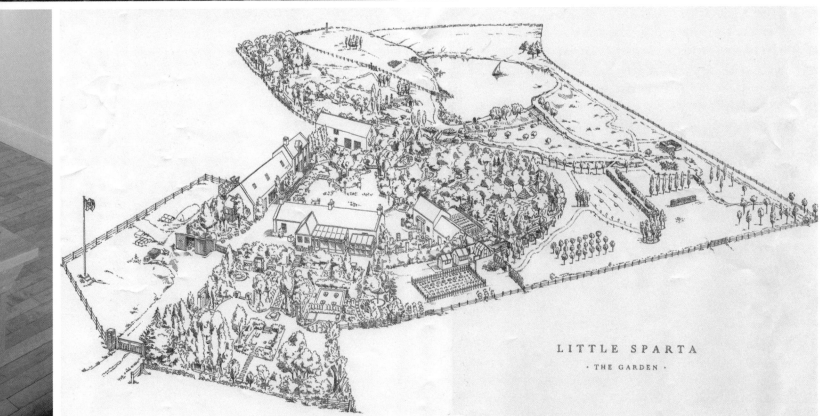

Thierry De Cordier, *THE GRASS-EATER (listening to the landscape)*, 1997–2005. Partial view of the back in semi-profile. Property of the artist. Wood, rubber, wire netting, concrete, blackened blankets, paint, motor oil, air, and zinc bathtub. 57 x 110 ¼ x 55 ⅛ inches.

"While its most ideal location is in the high grass of my backyard, this garden-piece can primarily be perceived as an herbivorous. (…) In some way looking like the half of an enormous black-dressed skull, autistic and without an entrance, this somber sculpture—which, I must say, was inspired by the tumorous head of my father—is a totally absurd and useless thing. Although, its emblematic significance lays in the fact that this container holds one's thoughts or inner-garden safely, a bit in the way a tabernacle does. (…)"

Thierry De Cordier, *THE GRASS-EATER (resting in my backyard)*, 1997–2005. Front view. Courtesy Marian Goodman Gallery, New York.

"I started the fabrication of this *Machin Célibataire* in 1997, but never reached its achievement. Today, the piece is in a moribund and heavily damaged state. And because of the great cold, I can only take it back in hand at the earliest next spring and finish it around mid-May. Just in time to put it on a ship to America. It is a strange feeling for me to imagine this black terrestrial thing floating over the ocean, on its way to the States....then reaching New York, brought to the Queens Museum to be watched like an ape during some months... After which it will come back in shame to the place where it really belongs!"

attest to his desire to fold literally into the image we see before us, the way the artist puts himself inside the work. Models of this sort of transubstantiation can be seen in his sculptural works, which have an immense presence—humble, at times olfactory, and physical like a giant piece of fruit. *Les Dos noirs* (The Black Backs), an ongoing series of works begun in the early 1990s, consists of rustic pavilions cloaked in organic materials, possibly conceived for thinking, working, gardening, or even cooking. While most serve various functions, they all protect a darkness found in the habitats of lower life-forms that exude a quiet romance, a soft lament. But some of these objects are gargantuan; one in particular, *The Grass-Eater*, 1997-2005, is a stubborn beast, medieval and Rablaisian, sitting there indefatigable in the garden from which it was created.

In the privacy of one's garden other gardens flourish. Born out of necessity to transcend place and time, the private garden of the artist grows only for visual feasting and intellectual stimulation. It is a place to escape into in order to find a place to get lost. Like all private gardens, the artist's garden is an obsession driven by seasonal waves to renew, accumulate, and perish over and over again, a never-ending project of immense satisfaction and grief, beautiful, demanding, and selfish.

NOTES

[1] All Noguchi quotes from Bonnie Rychlak, *Noguchi: The Bollingen Journey, Photographs and Drawings 1949-1956*, exh. brochure (New York: Noguchi Museum and Sculpture Garden, 2003), n. p.

[2] Ana Maria Torres, *Isamu Noguchi: A Study of Space* (New York: The Monacelli Press, 2000), 25 and 30.

[3] Ibid., 45-49. Ten years later Noguchi did a bronze model, *This Tortured Earth*, 1943, and in 1947 he created another model, *Memorial to Man*, later called *Sculpture to Be Seen from Mars*, which was destroyed. All are considered early earthworks projects.

[4] Gwen Chanzit, *From Bauhaus to Aspen: Herbert Bayer and Modernist Design in America* (Boulder, CO: Johnson Books; and Denver: Denver Art Museum, 2005).

[5] *Culture and Value*, a compilation of remarks, aphorisms, and musings on a variety of subjects—music, architecture, philosophy, religion—assembled from various notebooks and odds-and-ends manuscripts after Ludwig Wittgenstein's death, translated by Peter Winch and published by University of Chicago Press, 1980; this quote page 18e.

[6] The *Theatrum Botanicum* was written in 1640 by pharmacist John Parkinson (1567-1650) of London. It is an encyclopedia of medicinal plants, containing woodcuts and descriptions of more than 3,800 examples.

[7] Lothar Baumgarten, "Guide to *Theatrum Botanicum*," exh. brochure (Paris: Fondation Cartier, 1994), n. p.

[8] Dan Graham and Robin Hurst, "Corporate Arcadias," *Artforum*, December 1987, 68-72.

[9] Leslie Rose Close, "The Garden," in *Alfonso Ossorio: Congregations*, exh. cat. (South Hampton, NY: Parrish Museum of Art, 1997), 31.

[10] Klaus Kertess, "Eyewitnesses," in *Alfonso Ossorio: Congregations*, 17.

[11] *Derek Jarman's Garden* (Woodstock, NY: Overlook Press, 1996), 91.

[12] For a record of these "battles," see Yves Abrioux, *Ian Hamilton Finlay: A Visual Primer*, 2nd edition (London: Reaktion Books, 1992), 7-17.

[13] For an account of the relationship between Finlay and MacDiarmid, see Mark Scroggins, "The Piety of Terror: Ian Hamilton Finlay, the Modernist Fragment, and the Neo-classical Sublime," *Flash Point Magazine*, Web Issue 1 (Spring 1997); or see www.flashpointmag.com/ihfinlay.htm.

[14] Jane Brown, *Spirits of Place: Five Famous Lives in Their English Landscape* (London: Penguin Books, 2002), 245.

Work: Ecologies, Their Alternatives, and Schreber Gardens

Artists and nonartists alike would agree that an ecologically progressive garden requires collective, continued, and strenuous effort. Sometimes that effort translates into environmental fundamentalism, which can be uninspiring, even doctrinaire, to the public it hopes to engage. Several artists have averted this response by creating gardens that communicate the urgency of biodiversity in provocative ways, making the situation appear relevant to an increasingly diverse society. Their gardens stimulate poetic associations rather than brandish statistics, expressing interest via tangential (and occasionally deviant) means. These alternative ecologies have led us down garden paths that investigate subjects as far afield as human sexual behavior in natural settings and the correlation between the psychological world of the Schreber garden and political oppression and tyranny. While this expanded concept of work *in* and work *as* a garden may seem a leap, artists have probed into the complex histories of gardens to connect the real with the imaginary in provocative and demanding ways.

Alan Sonfist, among the first artists of his generation to take a public stand on the environment, grew up in the South Central Bronx and talks often about the hemlock forest in a vacant lot where he played as a boy. As a young man he translated that memory into a citywide proposal to restore and intervene in fifty neglected areas in New York City, yet today only one project has been fully realized—*Time Landscape*, a precolonial plot of land recreated on the northeast corner of LaGuardia Place and West Houston Street. Sonfist was a determined twenty-one-year-old when, in 1965, he asked the city for a lot that he would use to commemorate the original DNA of the island that had become Manhattan. In 1978, with the help of the Greenwich Village community and according to the artist's extensive research, Sonfist finally planted the twenty-five-by-forty-foot plot, contouring the ground in keeping with the original

Queens Museum of Art
Down the Garden Path

Chapter 1
Work: Ecologies,
Their Alternatives, and
Schreber Gardens

Alan Sonfist
Time Landscape, 1978
New York
Overhead views and detail

{69}

(clockwise from top right)
Robert Smithson
Floating Island to Travel Around Manhattan Island, 1970
Pencil on paper, 19 x 24 inches
Estate of Robert Smithson,
Courtesy James Cohan Gallery,
New York

topology of sandy hills and beech groves, perfectly replicating the environment of the island prior to European settlement in the seventeenth century. If the piece encapsulates a pre-urban condition, it is also a sign of the times. It was proposed when sound ecology was among the concerns for a generation waving every revolutionary flag. While it may be taken for granted by jaded neighbors or look suspicious to the accidental tourist now, *Time Landscape* was a coup for environmental activists and remains a symbol of its moment.[1]

Famous for his ambitious industrial interventions into the landscape rather than for an environmental or preservationist stance, Robert Smithson was deeply critical of the gardenesque and the "limbo of modern isms" it creates for sculpture sited outdoors. His rhetorical question "Could one say that art degenerates as it approaches gardening?" attests to his feeling that "the abysmal problem of gardens somehow involves a fall from somewhere or something."[2] Yet despite such declarations, Smithson *did* work with organic materials and he *did* conceive of several garden projects or proposals. In his famous essay "Frederick Law Olmsted and the Dialectical Landscape" (originally published in *Artforum* in February 1973), the artist identifies a dialectical relationship in Olmsted's preference for allowing nature to wreck the land over time, forming a picturesque rather than formal ideal. Olmsted, Smithson pointed out, "brought a Jeffersonian rural reality into the Metropolis."[3] He took a wasteland of squatter's parcels that was the site of Central Park and transformed it into "a succession of changing landmasses." Unlike Thoreau, "Olmsted made ponds, he didn't just conceptualize about them." The grand designer symbolized for Smithson the power of the man-made, of moving massive amounts of earth with machines to create an uncommon beauty offset by the restless mechanics of the city. Evoking Olmsted's project, Smithson dismissed the dream of an idyllic, isolated, landscaped estate in favor of working with devastation, waste, and neglect as assets in a new reality of nature. This essay, along with "A Tour of the Monuments of Passaic, New Jersey" and Smithson's theories on entropy, sites, and non-sites, are manifestos for a reconsideration of the natural world.[4]

In addition to offbeat sites in urban centers, Smithson was attracted to islands (other artists, notably Vito Acconci, have been drawn to them as well).[5] While studying at New York's Art Students League, he traveled to the island of Manhattan every day from his home in New Jersey. With his parents he vacationed on Sanibel Island, a small, ecologically important spit of land with a wildlife preserve in the Gulf of Mexico off Fort Myers, Florida. He also visited Robert Rauschenberg on neighboring Captiva Island when the older artist moved there in 1970. Later he settled on the lower west edge of Manhattan, where barges going up and down the Hudson served as a constant reminder that he lived on an island, a fact most of its residents forget.

In 1970 Smithson made a sketch titled *Floating Island to Travel Around Manhattan Island* in which he clearly labeled the New York City skyline, a tug, a barge, and on its deck a landscape one might consider a garden. This landscape includes, per the notations, earth, rock, moss, a path, a weeping willow, and "trees common to [the] N.Y. region." Given Smithson's involvement with Olmsted's position as a protomodernist landscape artist and his intimate knowledge of Central Park, I would propose that this landscape is not just any section of New York but in fact is a part of Central Park and an homage to Olmsted. In his Olmsted article, Smithson writes that the Ramble, a

Queens Museum of Art
Down the Garden Path

Chapter 1
Work: Ecologies,
Their Alternatives, and
Schreber Gardens

© Estate of Robert Smithson/
Licensed by VAGA, New York

*Panorama of the City of New
York* (detail), 1961–64
Designed by Lester Associates
Permanent installation,
Queens Museum of Art, New York

Collection of Queens Museum
of Art, New York
Photo: Eileen Costa

Acconci Studio (Luis Vera, design
and engineering; Jenny Schrider;
with the assistance of Lisa Albin)
Personal Island, 1992

Aluminum rowboats, soil,
grass, and trees
Installation view, the Floriade
festival, Zoetemeer, the
Netherlands
Courtesy of the artist

Acconci Studio (Vito Acconci,
Dario Nunez, Stephen Roe,
Peter Dorsey, Thomas Siegl,
Gia Wolff, Nana Wulffin,
Laura Charlton, Sergio Prego)
Mur Island, 2003
Mur River, Graz, Austria

(top left)
Gordon Matta-Clark
Islands Parked on the Hudson,
1970–71
Pencil, colored pencil, ink, and
marker on yellow legal paper,
8 ½ x 14 inches

section of the park that through neglect had begun to revert to its original state, "brought a primordial condition into the heart of Manhattan."[6] The Ramble, then, could well be the contents of the barge. If we follow Smithson's understanding of an island as a particle of another, larger particle, then *Floating Island* is precisely that. Sending a bit of Central Park in a circle around Manhattan, Smithson sought to stir up the primordial landscape, playing with scale and with the contraction of perimeter and center so prevalent in his work. *Floating Island* creates an ellipse around a rectangle, traveling like some cosmic mass around an even bigger cosmic mass. If it had been realized, it would have been an anomaly, a bit of ecological optimism, a little floating oasis amid a river of barges carrying the raw materials Smithson loved to play with—and, of course, amid those carrying garbage heading out to the Atlantic.[7]

Gordon Matta-Clark first met Smithson in February 1969, at the "Earth Art" exhibition curated by Willoughby Sharpe at the Andrew Dickson White Museum of Art at Cornell University in Ithaca, New York. Smithson, age thirty-one at the time, was invited to participate, and the twenty-six-year-old Matta-Clark had just graduated a year earlier.[8] Smithson's *Floating Island* and Matta-Clark's drawing known as *Islands Parked on the Hudson,* 1970–71, are strikingly similar—they present barges containing a landscape/garden against a skyline. On the other hand, they also feature several fundamental differences. While both works represent verdant mini-islands, Matta-Clark's barges are "parked" with a view of New Jersey; Smithson's barge was intended to travel around Manhattan, conveying his idea of a spiraling landscape, with the New York City skyline in the background.

In addition to this drawing of a garden on a barge on the Hudson, Matta-Clark made drawings of garden barges strung one after the other and connected by Japanese bridges, suggesting characters playfully linked together to create a sentence, not unlike a terrestrial counterpart of skywriting.[9] The barges themselves are filled with a variety of topiary trees. Jane Crawford believes that these energetic *Tree Forms,* which the artist drew roughly between 1969 and 1974, were designed in the shapes of the letters of his own name.[10] A possible meaning for these forms, the metaphysical identification with the topiary as pure natural energy metamorphosed, is an ancient and even Eastern theme—one not far from Smithson's series of fantastic, mythical drawings *Blind in the Valley of the Suicides* and *Birth in the Valley of the Suicides* (both ca. 1960–62), which Matta-Clark could have seen at Richard Castellane Gallery in New York in 1962.[11] Theirs was a friendship in which their closeness on a number of ideas was like intellectual sparring, playful and mutually beneficial.

In the past two decades, a younger generation has looked to the artists of the late 1960s and the 1970s, and to Smithson in particular, for inspiration in exploring the social spaces of landscape. For Tom Burr, this has meant observing human sexual dynamics in the context of green spaces, investigating how desire literally carves out its own path and creates alternative areas for unendorsed behavior. For *An American Garden,* 1993, Burr built a full-scale model of a small section of Central Park's Ramble inside another picturesque park, Sonsbeek, in Arnhem, the Netherlands, as part of the periodic sculpture exhibition there. Burr's garden is contained within a twenty-by-thirty-foot steel wedge—a nod to

Queens Museum of Art
Down the Garden Path

Chapter 1
Work: Ecologies,
Their Alternatives, and
Schreber Gardens

(bottom left)
Gordon Matta-Clark
Tree Forms, 1971
Pencil, ink, and marker on
paper, 18 ⅞ x 24 inches

(top right)
Gordon Matta-Clark
Tree Forms, 1971
Pencil, ink, and marker on
paper, 18 ⅞ x 24 inches
Image: Generali Foundation

(bottom right)
Gordon Matta-Clark
Tree Forms, 1971
Pencil, ink, and colored marker
on paper, 18 ⅞ x 24 inches
Image: Generali Foundation

All Matta-Clark images
© 2005 The Estate of Gordon
Matta-Clark. Courtesy Artists
Rights Society (ARS), New York

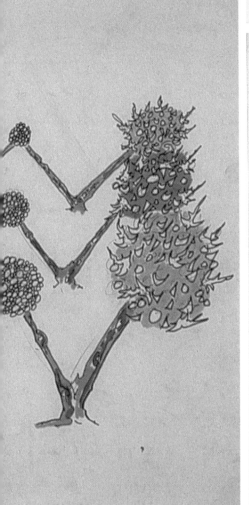

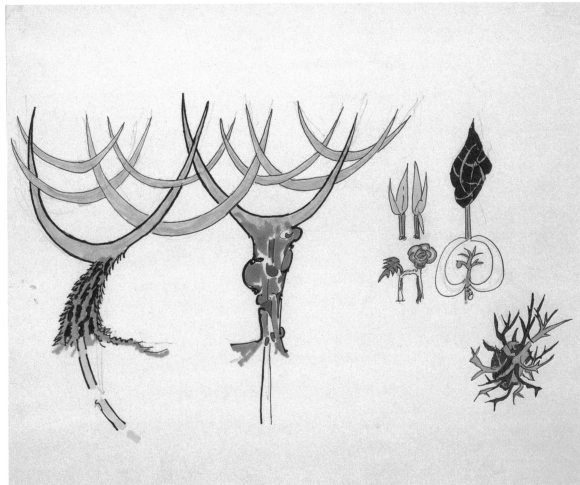

Queens Museum of Art
Down the Garden Path

Chapter 1
Work: Ecologies,
Their Alternatives, and
Schreber Gardens

(left and bottom right)
Tom Burr
An American Garden, 1993
Soil, plants, and plaques
Installation view and detail,
Sonsbeek 93, Arnhem,
the Netherlands

(top right)
Tom Burr
Jones Beach State Park, 1992
Lamp, sand, mixed media,
and table, 5 x 2 ½ x 2 ½ inches

Minimalism—and filled with the Ramble's exact composition of granite, rhododendrons, azaleas, and such. Informational signs are dispersed among the trees and bushes, but rather than describe the species that might be found here, the texts refer to gay cruising. One quotes Smithson's Olmsted article on the evolution of the Ramble from a dense, isolated wood designated for bird watching to a well-known trysting place: "The Ramble has grown into an urban jungle, and lurking in its thickets are 'hoods, hobos, hustlers, homosexuals', and other estranged creatures of the city." (Smithson himself drew this observation from John Rechy's 1963 novel *City of Night*.)

Like Smithson, Burr releases the potential of neglected places in nature by intervening in it. But where Smithson identified with the deviant element in nature, equating it with "a primordial condition into the heart of Manhattan,"[12] Burr turns the urban jungle into a *jardin d'amour*. The geometric configuration of *An American Garden*, with its strong sight lines, leads from the park's large Sonsbeek villa into the woods, where just beyond one can see the gay nightclub Entre Nous. Against the contradictory background of Holland's open society and its bourgeois conservativism, *An American Garden* points to the ancient, largely unacknowledged tradition of public parks being put to private use.

Mel Ziegler is another subscriber to the aesthetics of mobility. His *On Broadway*, 1980, a thirty-five-foot box trailer "painted on one side [with] orange and black stripes in order to match the orange Noguchi sculpture and the black Skidmore, Owings and Merrill building it was placed in front of,"[13] points to the often-skewed relationships between public art, architecture, and corporate clients. This work led in turn to *Instant Landscape*, 1984, a flatbed truck supporting fifty young fir trees intended to be parked in front of Artists Space on West Broadway in New York for one month. Labyrinthine city bureaucracy threatened the project during its preparation, but in the end *Instant Landscape* was finally installed, three weeks before Christmas in the burgeoning neighborhood of Tribeca. For many pedestrians, *Instant Landscape* was invisible, like so much public art in the city, but in this case because the piece was indistinguishable from hundreds of similar commercial vehicles selling Christmas trees. Only the most observant noticed that Ziegler's trees had their root balls bound in burlap with sphagnum and peat moss. This was no ordinary holiday display. Ziegler—originally from Pennsylvania, where forests of trees are cultivated solely for Christmas sales—created a cartoon of the disposability of nature. By the end of the month, birds had built nests deep within the interior of *Instant Landscape*, and a perplexed public sensed something "unnatural" in the midst of their concrete neighborhood.

Mark Dion's critiques of the agricultural industry have addressed its practices of selective propagation and disease control. Commissioned for the exhibition Artranspennine98, Dion's *Tasting Garden* at the Storey Gallery in Lancaster, England, is a living protest against what writer Michael Pollan identifies as monoculture: "Monoculture is where the logic of nature collides with the logic of economics; which logic will ultimately prevail can never be in doubt."[14] Concerned about the disappearance of diversity in vegetable and fruit production in the Western world, Dion set about creating a garden that would visualize the horrific possibilities if the powers that be continue to "perfect" species. In a sunken garden tucked behind the gallery that opens

Queens Museum of Art
Down the Garden Path

Chapter 1
Work: Ecologies,
Their Alternatives, and
Schreber Gardens

Mel Ziegler
Instant Landscape, 1984
Fir trees on flatbed truck
Installation view, Artists Space,
New York
Courtesy of the artist

Queens Museum of Art
Down the Garden Path

Chapter 1
Work: Ecologies,
Their Alternatives, and
Schreber Gardens

(right and center)
Mark Dion
The Tasting Garden, 1998
Storey Gallery, Lancaster, England
Garden view and details of
apple tree and plinth, stele, and
Arboroculturalist's shed
Courtesy of the artist

(top left)
Mark Dion
Three Apples, 1997
Pencil and gouache on paper,
18 ⅛ x 21 ½ inches
Courtesy Storey Gallery,
Lancaster, England

(center left)
Mark Dion
Pear, 1997
Pencil and gouache on paper,
21 ½ x 18 ⅛ inches
Courtesy Storey Gallery,
Lancaster, England

(bottom left)
Mark Dion
Plan for *The Tasting Garden*, 1997
Pencil on paper, 21 ⅝ x 24 inches
Courtesy Storey Gallery,
Lancaster, England

onto a grassy slope bordered by a crumbling stone wall, Dion planted several heirloom varieties of pear and apple trees. Paths crisscross between the trees and eventually to a hut, in which tools of the gardener's trade are stored inside a characteristically Dionesque archeological display. Not far beneath the surface of spiritual calm of the place is an implicit threat: The first food of our biblical consciousness, stripped of its biological uniqueness, will soon be obliterated to satisfy collective taste. In this garden, the apple and its sister pear are raised up on a pedestal, pumped up to steroidal proportions and gilded as if by Midas himself. With wry humor, Dion invites us to taste the difference in Lancaster.

The Hamburg-based artist collective Galerie für Landschaftskunst (Gallery for Landscape Art) shares some of Dion's philosophical and aesthetic interests. Founded by Till Krause and Anna Gudjónsdóttir, it has taken on scientific and educational projects on the garden, nature, the city, the suburb, and maps, often inviting collaboration with European institutions and like-minded international artists. The Galerie für Landschaftskunst is currently on hiatus as Krause takes a bicycle trip through Africa. For "Down the Garden Path," on behalf of the collective, Krause and his wife, Ute Schmiedel, have asked the people of Soebatsfontein, South Africa, to submit drawings both wishful and realistic toward revitalizing the arid, derelict area around the well at the center of their tiny village. (The project was supported by the German branch of BIOTA, a research and development organization for which Schmiedel works.) The drawings and designs will travel to Hamburg and Queens, ultimately, it is hoped, providing an impetus for change.

While Westerners generally separate home, work, religion, and health out of the garden, in indigenous cultures these elements play an integral, intricate, and balanced role there. A non-Western garden has specific significance that may not be apparent to outsiders; often the garden is at the center of the community, reinforcing human bonds.[15] This integration has driven Krause and Schmiedel's interest in working with remote and challenged communities, and is also the motivating force behind Lonnie Graham's heritage gardens, which provide spiritual and educational support for their surrounding communities, some as nearby as the outskirts of Philadelphia where he lives, others as far away as Kenya and the Ivory Coast. Graham's basic premise is that a garden supplies three essential needs: sustenance, medicine, and spiritual well-being. Additional benefits are its instructional value, its potential for community building, and its ability to inspire social and political tolerance. For instance, with *Enlightenment*, 2001, Graham helped create a garden in the back streets of Charleston, South Carolina, for the city's Wilmont Frasier Elementary School.[16] Caring for the garden changed the relationship between the students, the teachers, the parents, and the rest of the community, instilling a sense of responsibility and respect for others as well as an awareness of the fragility of life—all while furthering pedagogy in the social sciences, history, and geography. Graham begins his green projects with the intention that they become self-sustaining, but an additional motive is to inspire understanding across borders: Whenever financially possible he tries to partner one garden with another in a sister country, such as matching the Mexican community here in Queens with one in Mexico, or the African-American community in South Carolina with another in Kenya, so that real-life experience is attached to an understanding of how other cultures live.

Queens Museum of Art
Down the Garden Path

Chapter 1
Work: Ecologies,
Their Alternatives, and
Schreber Gardens

(spread)
Galerie für Landschaftskunst
*Soebatsfontein Fountain
Garden Project*, 2002–2004
Soebatsfontein village and
surrounding landscape,
South Africa
Photos: Ute Schmiedel

(center left)
Winning drawing for
*Soebatsfontein Fountain
Garden Project*, South Africa,
November 2004
Drawing: Anisca Cloete

(bottom left)
Drawing for *Soebatsfontein
Fountain Garden Project*, South
Africa, November 2004
Drawing: Jasmine Christiaans

Queens Museum of Art
Down the Garden Path

Chapter 1
Work: Ecologies,
Their Alternatives, and
Schreber Gardens

(left, top right, and center right)
Lonnie Graham
Enlightenment, 2001
Wilmont Frasier Elementary
School, Charleston, SC
Courtesy of the artist

(bottom right)
Lonnie Graham
African-American Garden, 1996
Muguga, Kenya
Courtesy of the artist

Spring 2004

Summer 2003

Fall 2003

Queens Museum of Art
Down the Garden Path

Chapter 1
Work: Ecologies,
Their Alternatives, and
Schreber Gardens

Christian Philipp Müller
Hudson Valley Tastemakers,
2003–2004
Bard College, Annandale-
on-Hudson, NY
Photos: Christian Philipp Müller

{85}

Spring 2003

Summer 2003

Summer 2003

Fall 2003

Spring 2004

Winter 2003

Summer 2004

(clockwise from top left)
Nils Norman
*Mobile Permaculture Container
Being Installed on an Occupied
Schrebergarten* (detail), 1996
Mixed media on pedestal,
19 ½ x 24 ½ x 12 ¼ inches
Private collection

Where Graham has taken his garden projects around the world, Christian Philipp Müller has focused on a single location: the Hudson River valley in New York state. *Hudson Valley Tastemakers* was a commissioned project funded by the nonprofit organization Minetta Brook that Müller began by researching the region's agriculture. Finding a small but growing fringe of producers interested in reclaiming the fertile land along the valley for a diverse selection of indigenous crops, he set about promoting their interests with a series of events that included eating, drinking, and otherwise reveling in the local bounty in a setting centered around a temporary artwork akin to a soil graph of the region. A one-hundred-foot-long minimalist steel wedge a foot and a half wide at its base and increasing to four feet wide at the top, the sculpture contained soil samples from six surrounding counties in which heirloom plants like golden purslane, calendula, oracle, lamb's quarters, and Shaman's blue corn, as well as Asian greens, are now being either successfully reintroduced or introduced for the first time as an experiment to diversify.[17] The first manifestation of the project, which took a year to plan and lasted one season, took place 2003–2004 at Bard College, whose campus overlooks the valley, and brought growers together with the local community, the college, and art-world city folk.

At the invitation of Diane Shamash, director of Minetta Brook, and the Powdermaker Hall Art Acquisition Committee, Müller held another food fete in fall 2004 at Queens College in New York City. In *Spice Up (Powdermaker Hall)*, created with students and faculty, the artist wrought names of food-bearing plants in porcelain enamel letters on the walls of the newly built dining hall, inscribing three global staples—corn, rice, and potatoes—and laminating images of spices onto eleven oval tables surrounded by stools. He rearranged the furniture in three student lounges, where students sit and casually eat. *Spice Up* celebrates the rich array of cultures and tastes that makes up this college community, which reflects the diversity of the borough of Queens itself, where some 170 languages and dialects are spoken.

London-based artist Nils Norman creates theoretical proposals in the form of models, posters, and tongue-in-cheek development plans for the green conversion of politically exploited or economically challenged sites such as Stuyvesant Place and Tompkins Square Park in New York, the prefabricated village of Tornitz in the former East Germany, and a roundabout in Bristol, England. His *Gerard Winstanley Radical Gardening Space Reclamation Mobile Field Center and Weather Station Prototype*, 1999, an itinerant self-propelled library on a bicycle, complete with solar-powered photocopy machine, makes the rounds of schools, museums, and town squares, informing and amusing people on such subjects as gentrification, radical gardening methods, and self-sufficient energy sources. Its namesake Winstanley (1609–1660) was a freeman of the Merchant Taylors' Company who lost his business during England's Civil War, spurring his fight for collective land ownership, for which he was persecuted. In a similar vein, Norman's *Geocruiser*, 2001, a tour bus that runs on vegetable oil, is outfitted with pro-environment libraries and laboratories, an art gallery, a video archive, a greenhouse, and a wormery. His advocacy for alternative energy production and self-sustaining land use has led to wonderfully complex composting and recycling models and graphic displays such as 2001's *Edible Forest Garden Park* ("utilizing all available space for maximum organic yield potential") and *Moltkestr 91/95*, 1996, a plot of land slated for redevelopment in Cologne

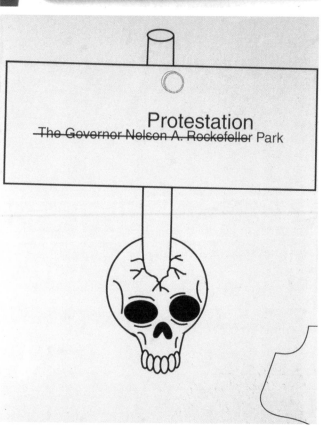

Queens Museum of Art
Down the Garden Path

Chapter 1
Work: Ecologies,
Their Alternatives, and
Schreber Gardens

Nils Norman
*The Gerard Winstanley Radical
Gardening Space Reclamation
Mobile Field Center and Weather
Station Prototype (New York
City Chapter)*, 1999
Bicycle, plywood, photocopy
machine, solar panel, books, and

weather-monitoring equipment,
86 x 138 x 76 inches
Courtesy Galerie Christian
Nagel, Cologne/Berlin

Nils Norman
Underground Agrarians
(detail), 1997

Mixed media
Courtesy Galerie Christian
Nagel, Cologne/Berlin

Nils Norman
*Proposed Occupation,
Resdesign, Renaming, and Reuse
of Nelson A. Rockefeller Park,*

Battery Park City, New York
(two details), 1999
Inkjet print, 72 x 49 ½ inches
Courtesy Galerie Christian
Nagel, Cologne/Berlin

that will instead become an organic vegetable exchange for produce grown in empty lots throughout the area.

Known for her minimalist forms in natural materials—moss mounds, cylinders made of meadows, convex cones of grass—Meg Webster often drifts away from making objects to making garden installations with a mission. She has created astonishing aquatic gardens, wetlands, and flowering earthworks for galleries and museums all over the United States, but her conviction that derelict urban spaces benefit from unofficial gardeners in the community has driven Webster's most precious and fragile garden to date—on the roof of the Brooklyn building where she keeps her studio. Threatened by lawsuits that will eventually lead to its dismantling, this 3,000-square-foot bit of meandering sylvan real estate is a sampler of bigger dreams to embrace every neglected spot in the city with green potential. Webster's naturalistic garden is home to a pond of koi and opportunistic pigeons as well as rescued beech trees, abandoned tea roses, and volunteer daylilies—a happy family of orphaned species living a motley but copasetic existence, all within eye- and earshot of the Williamsburg Bridge.

Brazilian artist, musician, horticulturalist, and environmental activist Roberto Burle Marx wondered why so few gardeners did not consider themselves artists.[18] Peter Fischli and David Weiss may have thought the reverse when they set out to create *Garten*, a mix of flowers and vegetables planted along the river Aa for 1997's Skulptur. Projekte in Münster. *Garten* was a simple kitchen garden and a makeshift toolshed, the kind one often sees along rivers and railroad tracks on the outskirts of European towns. There is nothing particularly aesthetic about the shed, which comprises of a sheet tied to two poles; utensils are scattered about; chicken wire is wrapped around plants animals favor—altogether a typical garden. Or not? Most gardeners are neat in order to maximize yield, so we are tipped off by discarded tools and lax maintenance that this garden is only quasi-horticultural. But if one spends time there, the notion of what is ordinary slowly gives way to the unusual and astonishing. The symphony of crickets and tree frogs starts its prelude; one by one these miniature actors make their appearance in this *theatrum botanicum*, and nature's opera begins, imperceptible to the impatient, or those too busy looking for art.

As an offshoot of *Garten*, Fischli and Weiss produced a sequence of seamlessly shifting untitled indoor projections, photographic images of flowers and fruit taken from a bumblebee's point of view. The projections envelop us from all sides; the magnitude of the flowers dwarfs us in hyperreal color and a sexual profusion of stamens and petals, overwhelming us with almost sickly beauty. An experience so intense prompts the question: Are we drawn to flowers inherently or because of an established cultural attitude toward them? Such is the "botany of desire," to borrow Pollan's term—the nature-culture conundrum so vividly represented in Fischli and Weiss's *Garten* project.

In 1989, intrigued by the possibility of using plants to pull toxins out of contaminated soil, Mel Chin joined forces with Dr. Rufus Chaney of the U.S. Department of Agriculture, who had tried in vain to pitch the idea to the government. Together they cooperated on what Chin refers to as a sculpture, though it's equally as much a garden. After a long nationwide site search, during which National Endowment for the Arts funds were granted, revoked,

Queens Museum of Art
Down the Garden Path

Chapter 1
Work: Ecologies,
Their Alternatives, and
Schreber Gardens

(left)
Meg Webster
*Roof-Garden Growing Beds with
Trees and Tomatoes*, 1989–2005
Soil, trees, roses, and tomatoes,
35 x 50 x 20 feet
Installation view, Brooklyn, NY
Courtesy of the artist

(right)
Meg Webster
Roof-Garden Pond, 1998–2005
Pond, wetland plants, koi, soil,
and pump, 25 x 25 x 4 feet
Installation view, Brooklyn, NY
Courtesy of the artist

{89}

Queens Museum of Art
Down the Garden Path

Chapter 1
Work: Ecologies,
Their Alternatives, and
Schreber Gardens

(left)
Meg Webster
*Roof-Garden Growing Beds with
Trees and Tomatoes*, 1989–2005
Soil, trees, roses, and tomatoes,
35 x 50 x 20 feet
Installation view, Brooklyn, NY
Courtesy of the artist

(right)
Meg Webster
Roof-Garden Pond, 1998–2005
Pond, wetland plants, koi, soil,
and pump, 25 x 25 x 4 feet
Installation view, Brooklyn, NY
Courtesy of the artist

Queens Museum of Art
Down the Garden Path

Chapter 1
Work: Ecologies,
Their Alternatives, and
Schreber Gardens

(bottom left, top center,
and bottom right)
Peter Fischli and David Weiss
Garten (Garden), 1997
Installation views, Skulptur.
Projekte in Münster, 1997
Courtesy Matthew Marks
Gallery, New York

(top left, bottom center,
and top right)
Peter Fischli and David Weiss
Untitled, 1997–98
Inkjet prints, 29 ⅛ x
42 ⅛ inches each
Courtesy Matthew Marks
Gallery, New York

and eventually reinstated, *Revival Field* was installed in 1991 on Pig's Eye, a fenced-in toxic landfill in Saint Paul, Minnesota. *Silene cucubalus, Thlapspi caerulescens*, fescue, and romaine lettuce were tested for their ability to absorb and contain substantial amounts of toxic metals and minerals such as cadmium and zinc. The initial project, ended in 1993, continues today on poisonous plots in Pennsylvania, the Netherlands, and Belgium. While all gardens are in a sense recyclable, *Revival Field* has become a model for a remedial garden in which toxic waste can be turned into wealth. Artists and scientists alike hope that the cost of green remediational processes can be recovered from recycled metals; several major international companies are banking on it.

Recently, Chin has turned his attention to another kind of garden, one that levels the playing field between people from different walks of life. Like many U.S. cities, Austin, Texas, is divided between the haves and the have-nots. Property and real-estate values, climate, and a booming local economy have made Austin both one of the fastest-growing and most economically diverse cities in the United States. Always concerned with the political injustice that comes with financial inequality, Chin proposed a garden in 2004 for the city's Jack S. Blanton Museum of Art that would bring the disenfranchised closer to ivory-tower institutions in desperate need of new blood and fresh ideas. Currently Chin is working with landscape architect Peter Walker on the project, entitled *Reverb*, which comprises a verdant one-acre plot on the north side of the museum. This strip of lawn will contain high-tech replicas of eight natural sites familiar to locals as tourist destinations—in Chin's words, "'found landscapes' from the city of Austin, selected for their iconic presence."[19] In the real world these locations fall on either side of the Balcones Fault and I-35, the geological and sociological features that affect and mark the city's split in demographics. An audio component originating from the actual locations will accompany each recreated environmental landmark, "encouraging an atmosphere of curiosity, convergence, and discovery"[20] and providing shaded spots where people of diverse social, economic, and political backgrounds can meet on common ground.

Schreber Gardens

Daniel Gottlieb Moritz Schreber (1808–1861), the German physician and pedagogue, is well known for both his contributions as a social reformer and for the sadistic "reforms" he exercised upon his eventually psychotic and suicidal sons. *Memoirs of My Nervous Illness* (1903), the reflections of Daniel Paul, Schreber's youngest son, was a model for Sigmund Freud's study of paranoia and schizophrenia. The case led Freud to analyze other accounts of patriarchic oppression, such as E. T. A. Hoffmann's "Der Sandmann" (1815), a vivid tale of a child's bogeyman and the extension of its underlying pathology into adult madness—and, in retrospect, a prophecy of Teutonic terror.

Schreber is also the mind behind Schreber gardens, urban garden allotments introduced by the German government to assist the poor in the first half of the nineteenth century. In his Christian mission to improve the physical and psychological environment of working- and middle-class families, Schreber saw gardens as both therapeutic and functional. The concept of the Schreber garden later evolved into the *Volkspark* conceived by architects such as Leberecht Migge, who thought of these green spaces as "open-air facilities for sports and gymnastics, for dancing and swimming and other diversions." The *Volkspark* quickly evolved into the *Jugendpark*, which was

Queens Museum of Art
Down the Garden Path

Chapter 1
Work: Ecologies,
Their Alternatives, and
Schreber Gardens

(top)
Mel Chin (with Peter Walker)
Reverb, 2005-
Selecting "iconic" sites for
replication in Austin, TX
Photos: Mel Chin/Peter Walker
Partners

(bottom)
Mel Chin (with Dr. Rufus Chaney)
Revival Field, 1991-93
Toxic-metal-absorbing plants
Installation view and details,
Pig's Eye Landfill, Saint Paul, MN
Photos: Walker Art Center,
Minneapolis, MN

"to include certain new features: a central axial route for marching and parades, a field for military exercises, an open-air theatre, a camp site on the edge of the lake and, at the southernmost end of the park, residential quarters for soldiers returned from the war."[21] Migge, together with the director of urban planning for Berlin, set out to unite the park and the *Siedlung* (new housing developments), giving each of those who had bravely served their country a green place dedicated to rest and recreation. While the superpatriotic tenor of Migge's ideas for the *Jugendpark* seems dangerously close to those of the National Socialists, his truly experimental plans for city gardens and his "green movement" beautifully matched Weimar architecture.

With this social evolution of the Schreber garden in mind, we turn to Stan Douglas's "*Potsdamer Schrebergärten*" (1994), a series of fifteen photographs of garden allotments that read like a set of time capsules of German social history. Potsdam, a peripheral district of Berlin, shelters the private sanctuaries of hundreds of residents who keep Schreber gardens there. These miniature natural cosmologies silently represent all that is efficient and tightly knit in German culture. The tidy little squares are not the practical horticultural plots of the underprivileged but the petit-bourgeois answer to second-home ownership. Middle-class allotments provide a means to display a sense of self-imposed values, social status, and ambition. Pride and expressions of nationalism manifest themselves in choices of plants, techniques, and design.

The industrious look of the "*Potsdamer Schrebergärten*" photographs make a perfect foil for Douglas's double-track black-and-white 16 mm film loop *Der Sandmann* shot the same year (during which Douglas was on a residency in Berlin, Hoffmann's hometown). The film is set in the remains of a Schreber garden whose obvious ruin both foretells the failure of Germany's utopian vision for the coexistence of urban planning and green spaces and the systematic erasure of a "rural society of mythical times."[22] The scene is clearly staged in a studio, one of the famous yet (even during Douglas's filming) increasingly derelict Babelsberg film studios, also in Potsdam, where Fritz Lang and Marlene Dietrich worked in early German cinema. At the time of Douglas's investigation, both the film studio and the actual Schreber gardens were slated for demolition to make room for a housing development. Douglas uses Hoffmann's classic story as a structural and narrative point of departure from which to consider the modernist paradigm of urban renewal as it has played out in the twentieth century.

Hoffmann's "Der Sandmann" begins with a boy's fear of the eponymous creature, an ogre who throws sand in the eyes of children when they don't go to bed. This fear is transferred to Coppelius, a stranger who pays secret nightly visits to the boy Nathanael's father, creating a curiosity that when satisfied results in a trauma and its repression; Nathanael attributes his father's eventual death to this scopic moment of discovery. The complex psychological drama of Hoffmann's tale is concentrated in Douglas's film in a three-hundred-sixty-degree pan onto Coppelius, who lurks about a Schreber garden—a lumbering specter of the supernatural side of Teutonic culture. When "Der Sandmann" was written, the science of kitchen gardens had on some levels of society reached a kind of cult status. Social events were organized around harvest (as they still are), and gardeners employed rituals or "magical" practices toward the production of better yields. Douglas picks up on Hoffmann's almost medieval depiction of Coppelius as a shaman in his garden, while the delusional Nathanael, represented by the narrator of the film (seemingly touched by shades of Daniel Paul Schreber's insanity),

Queens Museum of Art
Down the Garden Path

Chapter 1
Work: Ecologies,
Their Alternatives, and
Schreber Gardens

Stan Douglas
*Garden Designed by
Lenne Halbinsel Meederhorn,
Sacrow,* 1994
C-print, 18 x 21 inches
From the series *"Potsdamer
Schrebergärten,"* 1994

{95}

conveys the fever of childhood anguish as he recounts being pursued by visions of his long-dead father, last seen by his son at the bellows with the evil alchemist Coppelius, representative of the old religion. The story of recurring terror and guilt is brought to bear on the history of the Schreber garden through Schreber himself, the fate of his sons, Hoffmann's own creative madness, and the horror of World War II. Douglas transposes this terror and guilt to the compulsion for change, the frenetic desire for the modern, and the threat of slum clearance with the promise of capitalism and commerce, profit and progress, that epitomizes a new order and threatens to root out the magic in the garden.

NOTES

[1] For more on *Time Landscape*, see www.nycgovparks.org and, in these pages, "A Conversation with Alan Sonfist."

[2] "A Sedimentation of the Mind: Earth Projects," in *The Writings of Robert Smithson*, ed. Nancy Holt (New York: NYU Press, 1979), 86.

[3] Subsequent quotations this paragraph are from "Frederick Law Olmsted and the Dialectical Landscape," in *The Writings of Robert Smithson*, 118.

[4] For "A Tour of the Monuments of Passaic, New Jersey" and writings on the concepts of entropy, site, and non-site, see *The Writings of Robert Smithson*.

[5] Acconci played with the idea in 1992, with a boat island commissioned by the Floriade festival, in the Netherlands. The form later developed into Acconci's *Mur Island*, 2003, a theater café in the river Mur in Graz, Austria. Ludger Gerdes did a similar piece, *Schiff für Münster* (Ship for Münster), in 1987.

[6] Smithson, "Frederick Law Olmsted," 127.

[7] Smithson proposed the project to Alanna Heiss, director of the Institute for Art and Urban Resources in New York, today's P.S. 1 Contemporary Art Center, but it was never realized. Heiss, conversation with the author, June 2005.

[8] Nancy Holt recalls that Matta-Clark lived not far from them on the lower west side of Manhattan by the Hudson River and would visit the older artist. At the end of 1969, Matta-Clark sent Smithson a fried, gold-leafed Polaroid photograph of a Christmas tree, which was shown in "Documentations," a group exhibition he was in at the John Gibson Gallery. Holt, conversation with the author, winter 2004.

[9] The idea of topiaries as forming pseudonyms for Matta-Clark was suggested to me by Jane Crawford, Matta-Clark's widow, in a telephone conversation, spring 2004.

[10] Crawford offers that Matta-Clark's interest in movable garden projects could have been inspired by a cross-country trip with Tina Girouard, Mary Heilmann, and Richard Landry during which he drew trees. Ibid.

[11] Eugenie Tsai, "Robert Smithson: Plotting a Line from Passaic, New Jersey, to Amarillo, Texas," in *Robert Smithson*, exh. cat. (Los Angeles: Museum of Contemporary Art, in association with Berkeley, Los Angeles, and London: University of California Press, 2004), 16.

[12] Smithson, "Frederick Law Olmsted," 127.

[13] Mel Ziegler, quoted in *Selections from the Artists Space Slide File* (New York: Artists Space, 1984), n. p.

[14] Michael Pollan, *The Botany of Desire: A Plant's-Eye View of the World*, trade paperback edition (New York: Random House, 2002), 231.

[15] See Michel Conan, "From Vernacular Gardens to a Social Anthropology of Gardening," in *Perspectives on Garden Histories*, Dumbarton Oaks Colloquium on the History of Landscape Architecture series, vol. 21 (Washington, DC: Dumbarton Oaks Research Library and Collection, 1999).

[16] This project was co-curated by Mary Jane Jacob and Tumelo Mosaka for the exhibition "Evoking History: Listening Across Cultures and Communities," on the occasion of the Spoleto Festival, Charleston, SC, 2001.

[17] The precursor to *Hudson Valley Tastemakers* was Müller's 2001 *Winter Garden*, commissioned by wine entrepreneur Alois Lageder for his vineyard in Tenuta Löwengang, Magré, Italy.

Queens Museum of Art
Down the Garden Path

Chapter 1
Work: Ecologies,
Their Alternatives, and
Schreber Gardens

(top)
Stan Douglas
*View of Zu Alten Zauche with
Plattenbauen Hochhauser and
the Twin Smokestacks*, 1994
C-print, 18 ½ x 36 ½ inches
From the series "*Potsdamer
Schrebergärten*," 1994

(bottom left)
Stan Douglas
*Private Homes Under
Renovation Beside Potsdam-
West Am Wildpark*, 1994
C-print, 18 x 21 inches
From the series "*Potsdamer
Schrebergärten*," 1994

(bottom right)
Stan Douglas
*Path Through "Berg Auf" Am
Pfingstberg*, 1994
C-print, 18 x 21 ½ inches
From the series "*Potsdamer
Schrebergärten*," 1994

{97}

[18] William Howard Adams, "Roberto Burle Marx: The Unnatural Art of the Garden," in *Roberto Burle Marx: The Unnatural Art of the Garden*, exh. cat. (New York: Museum of Modern Art, 1993), 14.

[19] From a legend on Mel Chin's concept/construction plans for *Reverb*, 2004. For example, "the Mt. Bonnell Stones and Bull Creek components will be cast stone replicas from molds taken from the actual sites. The Bull Creek element will feature a pond that will have water flowing in the same direction as found at the site. The massive boulder, balanced on the pool's edge, will appear to hover over the water."

[20] Mel Chin, conversation with the author, winter 2005.

[21] Marco De Michelis, "The Green Revolution: Leberecht Migge and the Reform of the Garden in Modernist Germany," in *The Architecture of Western Gardens* (Cambridge, MA, and London: MIT Press, 1991), 415.

[22] Michel Conan, "From Vernacular Gardens to a Social Anthropology of Gardening," 96.

Chapter 2
Commissioned Gardens

In 1993 I was asked to organize an exhibition for Sonsbeek, a park in the center of the city of Arnhem, the Netherlands. Past Sonsbeek exhibitions had consisted of sculpture in the park—with the exception of Sonsbeek 1972, titled *"Buiten im de Park"* (Out of the Park). That exhibition took place at the height of the Conceptual movement, and its curator, Wim Beeren, engaged artists to create projects throughout Arnhem and the rest of the country. As I put together the eighth Sonsbeek exhibition some twenty years later, I thought it was time to go outside of the park again; I invited thirty-eight artists to create work specifically for the park, the city, and the floodlands around it.

My experience commissioning projects in the public realm with Sonsbeek 93, and with the Queens Museum of Art exhibition "Crossing the Line" in 2001 (in which forty-eight artists created site-specific work for cultural and noncultural locations throughout Queens), directly influenced "Down the Garden Path: The Artist's Garden After Modernism." The idea of gardens seemed a perfect fit for the Queens Museum, facing the magnificent expanse of Flushing Meadows–Corona Park. Taking advantage of this location, "Down the Garden Path" is a two-tiered exhibition that extends outside the museum with five newly commissioned gardens by artists in Flushing Meadows and the nearby Queens Botanical Garden.

In spring 2003 we sent out a request for qualification, and two hundred applicants met our initial call. Of those, ten finalists were invited to present in person a proposal to the commissioning jury, and five of these were chosen for commissions. The six-member jury included Assistant Commissioner of Queens Parks Estelle Cooper; Queens Parks Designer Bill Gotthelf; Jennifer Ward Souder, Director of Capital Projects/Assistant Director at the Queens Botanical Garden; artist Mel Chin; Tom Eccles, Executive Director of the Public Art Fund; Queens Museum of Art Executive Director Tom Finkelpearl; and myself, Valerie Smith, Queens Museum of Art Senior Curator and Director of Exhibitions.

Ghada Amer

Happily Ever After is a wedding garden that spells out the title phrase. The individual letters, made of iron, are approximately five feet high and stand together in a thirty-foot-diameter circle. A hardy vine grows up the letters, covering them completely.

A circular bench made of teak is placed in the center. Couples are encouraged to use the garden to take their wedding pictures.

Ghada Amer
Happily Ever After, 2005
Digital images
Architect: Nicholas Bunning
Architecture and Design
Courtesy of the artist and
Gagosian Gallery

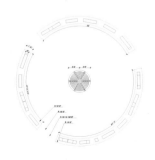

AXONOMETRIC VIEW

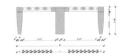

Lonnie Graham

Artist Lonnie Graham's commissioned project is a vegetable, flower, medicinal, herb, and meditative garden that will be planted and maintained by families from the Queens community through a joint partnership between Graham, the Queens Museum, members of the organization Mexicanos Unidos de Queens, the children and parents of P.S.14 and P.S.19 in Corona, and the families who enjoy Flushing Meadows–Corona Park. It will be used for educational purposes: to teach the children about plant growth, about good nutrition, and about their heritage by growing both local plants as well as those that are native to their home countries. The garden will serve as a vital link between the new American communities of Queens and the Queens Museum of Art.

Queens Museum of Art
Down the Garden Path

Chapter 2
Commissioned Gardens

Lonnie Graham
Jardines Gemelos de las Americas, 2005
Flushing Meadows-Corona Park,
New York, May 2005
Courtesy of the artist

Dave McKenzie and Anissa Mack

As part of *It's a Small Float...*, five small "floats" attached to the backs of bicycles are made available for public use; people may borrow them individually, or groups and families may use them to create their own small parade. Each float-on-a-bike consists of a bicycle pulling a wagonlike cart filled with real and artificial flowers, streamers, and flags and outfitted like a typical parade float. When not in use, the small floats cluster around a larger, stationary float that serves as a visual focus for the artwork. When the small "satellite" floats are elsewhere in the park, the central float allows people to climb aboard and be a beauty queen, mayor, high-school kid, Cub Scout, or whichever voice of the community they choose. The satellite floats can travel to any corner of the park, maximizing the impact on park life. This mobility allows people to see the floats not only as sculptural objects but also as memories, stirring recollections of parades and other events that they have witnessed throughout their lives.

Queens Museum of Art
Down the Garden Path

Chapter 2
Commissioned Gardens

Dave McKenzie and Anissa Mack
It's a Small Float…, 2005
Digital images
Courtesy of the artists

{105}

Franco Mondini-Ruiz

Thinking Green allows me to play with juxtapositions on a larger, more dramatic scale—a lowly, underappreciated Chia-inspired sculpture becomes a Rococo folly, an Easter Island monolith, an Olmec warrior head, a Disneyesque icon, a timely and friendly terra-cotta-and-grass reminder to love the earth, a good laugh, a nostalgic '70s journey, a poetic pun, a celebration of the pedestrian and the everyday, the expression of an artist who loves culture both high and low.

THINKING GREEN

A "Chia"-esque giant terra cotta colored fiberglass or plaster head sprouting live or artificial (as season permits) foliage hair

Queens Museum of Art
Down the Garden Path

Chapter 2
Commissioned Gardens

(left)
Franco Mondini-Ruiz
Final proposal for *Thinking Green*, 2005
Digital image
Courtesy of the artist

(top right)
Franco Mondini-Ruiz
Proposal for *Waiting for the Big One*, 2005
Digital image
Courtesy of the artist

(bottom right)
Franco Mondini-Ruiz
Proposal for *Pizza Lovers Garden!*, 2005
Digital image
Courtesy of the artist

{107}

WAITING FOR THE BIG ONE

Oversized bird garden house - maybe just a facade - need engineering expertise for safe hanging from metal pole camouflaged as tree -

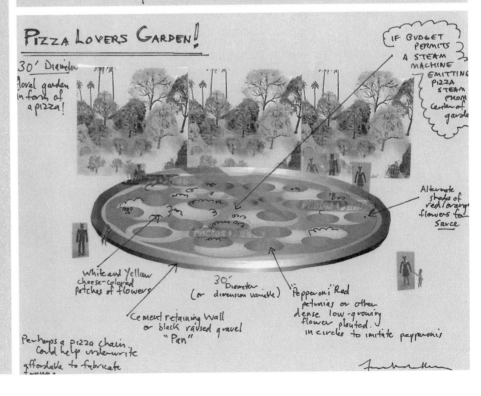

PIZZA LOVERS GARDEN!

Brian Tolle and Diana Balmori

Skid Rows is both a garden and an artistic process. Artist Brian Tolle and landscaper Diana Balmori will careen around a grassy two-acre expanse of the Queens Botanical Garden, doing doughnuts in a red Chevy pickup decorated with flower decals. With a custom-made tiller attached to the rear wheels, the truck will inscribe the earth while at the same time releasing yellow tick-seed and red poppy seeds. This revolutionary new method of low-impact cultivation, called direct sowing, challenges traditional planting techniques, which tend to disturb the soil's essential water- and nutrient-retaining capabilities. *Skid Rows* will create an unusual flower garden in the form of a two-and-a-half acre drawing, evoking famous European *parterre* gardening practices, developed in France in the late-sixteenth century by landscape architect Étienne Dupérac.

Queens Museum of Art
Down the Garden Path

Chapter 2
Commissioned Gardens

(left and center)
Brian Tolle and Diana Balmori
Skid Rows, 2005
Performance views,
Queens Botanical Garden,
New York, May 2005
Courtesy of the artists

(right)
Brian Tolle and Diana Balmori
Skid Rows, 2005
Digital images
Courtesy of the artists

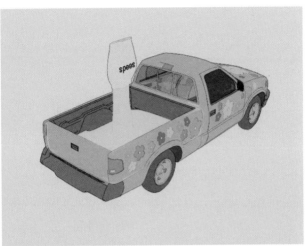

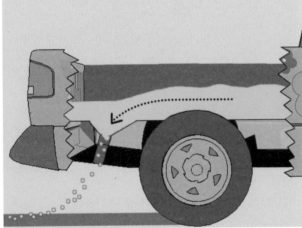

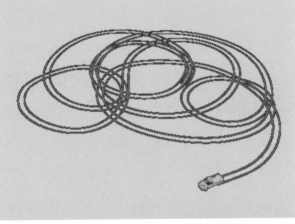

Chapter 3
Essays

People, Plants, and Prejudice
Julian Agyeman

It should come as no surprise to us that people can be prejudiced against plants. What is perhaps more surprising is that those who supposedly love them most, namely ecologists and conservationists, are the worst offenders. Nicholson notes that "conservationists are by tradition prejudiced against non-native plants. With few exceptions aliens are seen as detrimental to the wildlife interest of an area."[1] But just what are "alien" plants?

A classification of plants according to their origin and degree of persistence in the flora, from Gilbert:[2]

Native	Species that have arrived in the studied area by natural means without intervention, even unintentional, by man, from a source where the plant is native.
Alien	Species believed to have been introduced by the intentional or unintentional agency of man.
	1) Naturalized aliens (neophytes—new citizens). Introduced species which are naturalized in natural or seminatural habitats.
	2) Established aliens (epoekophytes). Introduced species which are established only in man-made habitats.
	3) Casuals (ephemerophytes). Introduced species which are uncertain in place or persistence.

The "traditional dogma"[3] and antipathy towards aliens is supported by leading UK urban ecologists Baines and Smart, who argue that, in nature conservation, "one of the basic principles is to reintroduce native species of British wildlife to towns and cities. Native plants tend to support a much greater variety of animal life than species introduced from other countries. Plants native to Britain are preferable to cultivars and varieties of exotic plants and trees so often used in urban landscaping."[4]

But the language surrounding the "alien" and the sentiment behind that language can get uglier, more menacing, and downright racist. Nicholson notes of alien plants that "sometimes they are disliked simply because they are 'foreign' and therefore out of place in native plant communities."[5] Wright, in discussing conifers in the British landscape, notes that "they are . . . alien imports, plainly lacking the cultural credentials of the native broadleaf" and "like other immigrants these fir trees all look the same to the affronted native eye."[6] Fenton is even more direct: "Dislike of alien species is indeed similar to racial discrimination—wanting to preserve the culture and genetic integrity of one's own stock (a natural human failing). Alien species are welcome in strictly defined areas (gardens) but must not be allowed to pollute the native culture (the wider countryside)."[7]

This "philosophy," if it can be called that (or is it more correctly an ideology?), stems from work done on shrubs and trees in Britain by Southwood[8] and Kennedy and Southwood.[9] It showed that native British species, such as English oak, supported a greater diversity of insect species, at 284, than nonnative species such as sycamore, with 43. The "reanalysis," however, showed that the number supported by sycamore was close to other natives such as field maple with 51, hornbeam with 51, lime with 57, and rowan with 58.[10]

Aside from the ideological aspects, assessing "wildlife value" solely on the total number of species supported is not reliable, particularly in urban areas. Sycamore, a staple of urban areas in Britain (a country with only thirty or so native trees, none of which do very well in cities), supports an enormous biomass of its primary phytophagous (plant-eating) insect, the sycamore aphid, which has at least nine different predators and parasites, which are in turn devoured by other insects and birds. Morton-Boyd points out that it has bole cavities, a rich leaf litter, is a substrate for lichens, and produces abundant seed.[11] It is also a prolific producer of early nectar, which attracts bees. However, because of its ability to attract only a limited *diversity* of wildlife, it is castigated by many urban conservationists as being of little value and is subject to "syccie bashing,"[12] i.e., "removal" from sites by zealous urban conservation managers and volunteers. This offensively named practice ("paki bashing" is the beating of Pakistanis or other Asians in Britain) ignores the huge biomass that sycamores can support. Indeed, Barker rightly argues that "it may not be the numbers of species which is significant but the biomass which is supported. Sycamore, for instance, supports a larger biomass of invertebrates than Oak or Alder do and to a bird it matters less that the insect it has eaten is common or rare than that it has eaten the thing at all."[13]

Unthinking actions by urban conservation managers and volunteers, which are part of the British urban conservationist ethos and of some Urban

Wildlife Groups, do not end with the sycamore. Gilbert notes that

> Japanese Knotweed suffers from a poor image. Knotweed bashing is taking over from scrub clearance as the standard task for conservation volunteers. It has a bad press. It must be one of the most hated plants in Britain with Giant Hogweed and Sycamore. But hang on a minute, are there "good guys" and "bad guys" in nature? Don't we just have communities of plants and animals interacting in a neutral manner which in trading countries like the UK are necessarily going to contain introduced species?

He continues by adding that Japanese Knotweed "is a bit of a whizz. It flowers late . . . [and] it provides an abundant and easily accessible source of nectar and pollen for all manner of insects."[14]

Clearly, the native/alien debate within British ecology and conservation is not as simple as assigning the label "good" to native and "bad" to alien, especially in urban areas. Of the several thousand species in Britain which today fall into one of Gilbert's categories of alien,[15] relatively few present a problem to the native flora, especially in urban areas. Even some of those that *apparently* do may be more related to conservationists' campfire myths than good ecological science.[16] If ecologist and conservationist language regarding aliens is clumsy and undiplomatic, British journalists such as Schoon take us to new heights. In the well-respected, left-leaning *Independent on Sunday*, he attempted to popularize the native/alien debate by appealing to people's xenophobia. His choice of archaic and pejorative phrases is wide ranging and unguarded. One can only assume that his sources (ecologists?) fed him their own prejudices, which he then adapted into emotional populism.[17]

Schoon talks of "encroaching foreigners," "running riot," "ferocious, fast growing foreign plants," "the villainous and the benign," "acceptable aliens," "staggering penetration," "ruthlessly ousting the natives," "pink and green Japanese terror," and plants which "brutalise the native flora." This undisguised xenophobia, including sexual metaphor ("staggering penetration"), is an indication of the depth of feeling (and fear) that the issue raises.[18]

North of Hadrian's Wall, *Scotland on Sunday* ran an article entitled "Ethnic cleansing in woods roots out non-Scots pines" in which the Forestry Authority (a government agency) was cutting down trees because it was deemed that they were not "sufficiently Scottish in origin."[19] Similarly, the *Independent on Sunday* ran a story with the headline "Hitler law used against UK Oaks" in which it was argued that a European Union Directive on forest reproductive material, derived largely from the German Forest Race Law of 1934, ensured that nurseries could "breed only from perfect and pure-bred examples of a species."[20] Not to be outdone, the right-leaning *Daily Mail* ran an article titled "Beast of the moor is hacked to death" about efforts to halt rhododendron encroachment on British moorlands.[21]

The depth of fear surrounding "the alien" is sensationalized, even by the quality press in Britain. However, it is well documented by Doughty,[22] who, like Fenton,[23] takes the argument to its logical conclusion by noting the popular comparison in the nineteenth-century United States between alien plants or animals and human immigrants. Doughty discusses the feelings of Americans about the immigration of the English house sparrow into the US in the nineteenth century, describing beliefs that "sparrows and immigrants had 'low morals,' reproduced at amazing rates, and appeared to be plotting and conspiring to exploit the United States at the expense of native-born Americans. In contrast, native birds were clean, tidy and hardworking who preferred country living and fulfilled the 'yeoman myth.'"[24] Doughty continues by noting that, according to Berrey's *American Thesaurus of Slang*, "Irishmen were also nicknamed sparrows because they were so numerous and prolific."[25]

Niemann summarizes the prevalence of xenophobia in conservation when he states, "Properly controlled elsewhere in society, overt racism runs unfettered throughout environment-speak, as we are taught about the need to promote native species and remove aliens which are bad for wildlife."[26] Yarrow agrees: "Am I the only person to think this is a nonsense reflecting our island mentality and a politically correct form of xenophobia? Racial and religious discrimination is no longer acceptable, yet substitute 'people' for plants in a sentence such as 'plants of non-local, and especially foreign, origin are no longer acceptable' and you see what I mean."[27]

Challenging the Traditional Agenda

Several authors have challenged the implications of the divisive traditional ecologist and conservationist agenda, in terms of the native/alien debate.

Egler notes that the native/alien debate is "eminently emotional, rather than serenely scientific,"[28] while Lugo, like Gilbert,[29] argues that "the eradication of species is not as simple as assigning evil qualities to exotic species and benevolent qualities to natives." Lugo continues that "responsible ecological stewardship requires an open mind to all species and the roles they play. It is a mistake to judge a species by its origin (exotic or native). We no longer live in a pristine world, if such a world ever existed. We are moving towards a landscape where human influence will be pervasive. All species have a role to play."[30]

Barker goes further than Lugo: "In Britain we often qualify the term 'wildlife,' whatever we understand by it, by distinguishing 'native wildlife' from 'alien wildlife'. I would contend that this particular distinction in Britain is not only indefensible to an ecologist but also lies at the root of an unhelpful nature conservation mythology which encourages activity without any thought about why that activity is taking place."[31]

Common Ground, a group that links arts and culture to conservation, also challenges the traditional ecologist and conservationist agenda. They rightly argue that it is "local distinctiveness" (i.e., what makes a place special) that is important, in this case in terms of plants, irrespective of their origins. They note that

> you can still tell that you are in Bournemouth and Poole from the legacy of the Victorians who started planting Scots and Maritime Pines in the 1800s. Later, Rhododendrons (R. ponticum) were introduced and spread quickly on the poor sand and gravel. In one year, in the late 1920s, over ten thousand pines were planted in Bournemouth by the local authority. As a result, Bournemouth looks as if it has grown up in a pine wood. It has a unique identity.[32]

They continue that "it is the predominant plants, the locally typical that characterise places, seldom the rare. These may be native or introduced—aubretia, campanula, snow in summer, valerian in the walls, the daffodils that grow in the fields and verges around Dymock or the hardy fuschia hedges in Cornwall."[33] This is a challenge to both the native/alien debate and to the dominance of scientific and rarity criteria in assessing the importance of sites.

Trepl, writing from a central European perspective, provides a useful insight into attitudes to aliens, or "neophytes." He differentiates between two approaches to research into this area. One was through natural science, with "botany or plant geography as a biological discipline," and the other, "in which botany was a part of geography," was a cultural-science approach.[34] In German, the latter approach is the *Kulturwissenschaften* (cultural-ecological) approach to the study of the anthropogenic migration of plants (hemerochory).

This approach, he argues, was developed in the nineteenth century. It was linked "not with general natural laws but with individualities (e.g. 'folk,' 'spirits' of nations, state, country)."[35] It is thus an ideological, patriotic, and nationalistic approach. Trepl offers similar sentiments to those of Lowe,[36] who notes that "from the turn of the century period comes an aesthetic and spiritual identity with the wild, strong anti-urban and anti-industrial sentiments, and a sense of stewardship, associated on the one hand with an appreciation of the web of life and its fragile balance, and on the other hand with a patriotic attachment to the indigenous flora and fauna."

Trepl notes that, in an extension of Fenton's and Doughty's arguments, that "perhaps the emphasis on the 'aggressiveness' of successful alien species (usually seen as being genetically determined) also has such an ideological background"[37] and that

> the real problem is the conservative bias inherent in 'cultural-science' approaches, which is structural and by no means merely the result of the private opinions of individual researchers.... The question is whether this problem of structural conservatism has a different weight now compared to the period of historic 'Kulturwissenschaften' in the late 19th century and the beginnings of the 20th i.e. whether these, or their surviving elements, have also altered their political, social and cultural position.[38]

The writings of authors such as Kohn (*The Race Gallery*)[39] and Herrnstein and Murray (*The Bell Curve*)[40] suggest that they have not.

NOTES

1 B. Nicholson, "Native versus alien," *London Wildlife Trust Magazine*, Winter 1987-88, 4 (unpaginated).

2 O. L. Gilbert, *The Ecology of Urban Habitats* (London: Chapman & Hall, 1989).

3 Nicholson, "Native versus alien," 4.

4 C. Baines and J. Smart, *A Guide to Habitat Creation*, Ecology Handbook no. 3 (London: GLC, 1984): 6.

5 Nicholson, "Native versus alien," 4.

6 P. Wright, "The disenchanted forest," *The Guardian Weekend*, November 7, 1992, 6.

7 J. Fenton, "Alien or native?" *Ecos* 7 (1986): 22-30.

8 T. R. E. Southwood, "The number of species of insect associated with various trees," *Journal of Animal Ecology* 30, no. 1 (1961): 1-8.

9 C. E. J. Kennedy and T. R. E. Southwood, "The number of species of insects associated with British trees: A re-analysis," *Journal of Animal Ecology* 53 (1984): 455-78.

10 Ibid.

11 J. Morton-Boyd, "Sycamore: A review of its status in conservation in Great Britain," *Biologist* 39, no. 1 (1992): 29-31.

12 G. Barker, "Which wildlife? What people?" *Urban Nature* 2, no. 1 (1994): 16.

13 Ibid., 15.

14 O. L. Gilbert, "Japanese knotweed: What problem?" *Urban Wildlife News* 11, no. 3: 1.

15 Gilbert, *Ecology*.

16 See Morton-Boyd, "Sycamore"; Gilbert, "Japanese knotweed"; and Barker, "Which wildlife?"

17 N. Schoon, "The barbarians in Britain's back yards," *Independent on Sunday*, May 17, 1992.

18 Ibid.

19 H. Davidson, "Ethnic cleansing in woods roots out non-Scots pines," *Scotland on Sunday*, October 30, 1994.

20 R. North, "Hitler law used against UK Oaks," *Independent on Sunday*, November 20, 1994, 7.

21 "Beast of the moor is hacked to death," *Daily Mail*, January 6, 1995.

22 R. Doughty, "The English sparrow in the American landscape: A paradox in nineteenth century wildlife conservation," *Research Papers* 19 (Oxford: School of Geography, 1978): 1-36.

23 Fenton, "Alien or native?"

24 Doughty, "The English sparrow," 28.

25 Ibid., 28.

26 D. Niemann, "A greater community for conservation," *The Wildlife Trust Magazine*, published by Beds and Cambs Wildlife Trust, no. 5 (1992): 10.

27 C. Yarrow, "Make our flora multiracial," *Horticulture Week*, June 16, 1994, 21.

28 F. E. Egler, "The nature of naturalization," *Recent Advances in Botany* (Toronto: University of Toronto Press, 1961): 1342.

29 Gilbert, "Japanese knotweed," 1.

30 A. Lugo, "More on exotic species," *Conservation Biology* 6, no. 1: 6.

31 G. Barker, "Which wildlife?" 14.

32 Common Ground, *The Art of Gentle Gardening: Thoughts on Linking, Plants, People and Places* (London: Common Ground, 1995): 3.

33 Ibid., 9.

34 L. Trepl, "Research into the Anthropogenic Migration of Plants and Naturalisation," in H. Sukopp and S. Hejny, eds., *Urban Ecology* (The Hague: Academic Publishing, 1990): 75.

35 Ibid., 81.

36 P. Lowe, "Values and Institutions in British Nature Conservation," in A. Warren and F. B. Goldsmith, eds., *Conservation in Perspective* (Chichester, England: Wiley, 1983): 349.

37 Trepl, "Research," 88.

38 Ibid., 93.

39 M. Kohn, *The Race Gallery: The Return of Racial Science* (London: Jonathan Cape, 1995).

40 R. Herrnstein and C. Murray, *The Bell Curve: Intelligence and Class Structure in American Life* (New York: Simon and Schuster, 1996).

The Willed Garden
Jamaica Kincaid

1.

The Willed Garden is enclosed in the North by a forest of Maples and Larch, in the East by a wild grassy meadow that is home to a large family of woodchucks, in the South by a home for children whose parents were not able to care for them properly, and in the West by the setting Sun. Those are the four borders of The Willed Garden.

2.

Within the borders of The Willed Garden there does not exist a river that then divides and becomes four branches. Within the borders of The Willed Garden, water, coming from a place I do not know, seeps out of the surface of the earth, making large parts of The Willed Garden into a wetland. The wetland is protected by laws, enforced by the government, local and Federal, and so cannot be tended in any way by my imperfect hand.

3.

Within the borders of The Willed Garden there does not exist a river that then divides and becomes four branches. Within the borders of The Willed Garden, the plumber has attached many feet of pipes made of copper and through these pipes The Willed Garden receives an essential necessity and aspect of its existence. So, just so, is The Willed Garden, water flows through it from the North Bennington Water Department; water that is collected from rainfall in a natural spring above the Village of North Bennington.

4.

Within the borders of The Willed Garden can be heard the baying and yelping and cries of wild dogs, and the wise sorrowing of owls, and the sick screeching of cats mating, and the winged mice flying, and the white-tailed deer swallowing the ripening buds of Rhododendron, and the stone-seed fruit trees being consumed by fire blight. Within the borders of The Willed Garden is a small hell.

5.

The name of the plumber who sets up the various sets of pipes and other sound contraptions to make possible the presence of water in The Willed Garden is sometimes Bob, sometimes Greene, sometimes Harhan, sometimes Zeke. The name of the plumber is never Aaron or Adam, for they are listed first in the alphabetical order of the phone book, and anyone in need of a plumber, whether for the garden or the kitchen or the bathroom, will find Aaron and Adam listed in the phone book ahead of those other plumbers who are in The Willed Garden.

6.

And is there a Willful Gardener within the borders of The Willed Garden? Yes, there is. In the morning, she stands near the East Border, drinking a cup of Coffee. In the evenings she walks towards the West Border as she drinks a Martini. Coffee and Martini, as morning and evening, make up the Border of her day. Without such Borders, The Willed Gardener would be lost, The Willed Gardener would not be a gardener at all but instead would be a lost soul in a desert.

7.

Within the borders of The Willed Garden The Willful Gardener has planted many trees that are pleasing to see when they are in bloom. The fruit of these trees are pleasing in taste but only to birds, for The Willful Gardener has willed that so. She said, to herself, I will buy the fruit I will eat from Jack at Walker Farms, I will plant only trees whose blooms are pleasing to the eye. With this resolution The Willful Gardener bows down before her own self and such idolatry is pleasing to her.

8.

The Willful Gardener stands on the terrace. From the terrace can be seen the not-to-be-tampered-with wetlands, the old worn-down mountains, the diseased apple orchards. Yet these three entities do not exist by themselves, they make up a delicate set of interrelated spheres in which are contained the places where the cardinals live, the coyotes den, the path the foxes take, the place where the deer sometimes spend the night. It is evening when The Willful Gardener is standing on the terrace and the sun has set over Albany. It is morning when The Willful Gardener stands on the terrace and the sun is rising forever. The Willful Gardener loves the morning and the sun forever rising. The Willful Gardener bows her head to the sun forever rising.

9.

In The Willed Garden lives a snake, or so thinks The Willful Gardener. She sees it, lying like a beautiful lamp's wick about to be lit, on the edge of the terrace, and among the clumps of Emerus, and among the Delphiniums, and among the smelly scrambling Codonopsis and among the Anemone rivularis and among the Peltiphyllum peltatum and among every other thing good to look at. A stroke of fear paralyses The Willful Gardener, for The Willed Garden is indeed inhabited by this slithering, tongue-darting vertebrate of which she is irrationally afraid. For the snake has no interest in her, is also afraid of her because her fear is so dangerous. When The Willful Gardener is afraid she calls a man who owns a gun and he kills whatever she is afraid of. All things living in The Willed Garden carefully monitor the degree of fear that is natural to The Willful Gardener.

10.

The Willful Gardener pauses. The Flowering Trees of every kind have bloomed and are overburdened with fruit. The birds shriek with delight as they eat the fruit and then fall with a soft thud to the ground, drunk from eating so much sweetness. The fox and her children make a feast of the birds.

"Freiheit in Grenzen"? Gardens as Places of Progress, Protection, and Persecution
Joachim Wolschke-Bulmahn

The title of this essay, *"'Freiheit in Grenzen'?"* ("Freedom Within Limits"?), is taken from a catalogue of private gardens for houses and villas published during the National Socialist period by landscape architect Hermann Mattern.[1] One common characteristic of many such gardens was the way they were sheltered from the outside world by walls, fences, and hedges. Was it the case that Mattern regarded freedom under National Socialism—when racism and anti-Semitism were actively encouraged, even required, by the state; when political dissidents and other groups were persecuted—as existing solely in one's own garden, protected from the generally hostile public sphere? This could be inferred from the catalogue's title, *"Freiheit in Grenzen."*[2] Did the garden become, under National Socialism, a refuge from the outside world, whose high, solid boundaries offered seclusion and hindered surveillance by the Gestapo, the block-warden party functionary, strangers, and neighbors?[3]

In what follows, addressing the question *"'Freiheit in Grenzen'?"* will encompass issues of gardens and freedom, progress, protection, and persecution in connection with National Socialism. The first part will take examples from progressive professional garden design to discuss the artistic freedoms that prevailed during the democratic Weimar Republic. The second part will address the possible significance of the garden for Jewish citizens as a place offering, temporarily, "freedom within limits." To conclude, a discussion of public parks will show how they were used by the National Socialists to persecute and discriminate against the Jewish population.

The Garden as an Expression of Artistic Freedom

In Germany during the Weimar Republic, an exceptional spirit of liberty in professional garden architecture circles prevailed, which expressed itself, for example, in multifarious experimental designs of gardens for private houses. As early as the *Kaiserreich* period, the profession had concerned itself intensely with progressive trends in the design of house and villa gardens. Renunciation of the stereotypical wholesale transfer of the landscape-garden style from feudal parkland to the markedly smaller domestic garden, and perceptions of the garden as a natural extension of indoor living space and the concomitant architectonic design of the garden, can be seen as the main characteristics of this period, lasting from about 1900 to the outbreak of the First World War.[4]

With the advent of the Weimar democratic republic, discussions within the profession in Germany on the design of gardens became even more intense and diversified. This is clearly reflected in the professional journals of the 1920s; countless articles by progressive garden architects such as Leberecht Migge, Hans Friedrich Pohlenz, Georg Bela Pniower, and Heinz Wichmann presented garden designs that experimented with modern trends in architecture and the arts and in which, for example, one can see consonances with the *Neues Bauen*, *Neue Sachlichkeit*, Expressionist, and Cubist movements. Art exhibitions and garden shows were the professional showcases for these design experiments.

A particularly interesting example of these trends is the *Sonderbare Garten* (Peculiar Garden; fig. 1) by Hans Friedrich Pohlenz.[5] Pohlenz was among the most enthusiastically experimental garden designers of the Weimar period, and designed the *Sonderbare Garten* for the Juryfreie Kunstschau Berlin (Berlin Unadjudicated Art Show) in 1925. Its very title was, as it were, part of the avant-garde manifesto, a provocation to some contemporary garden architects. The design clearly reflects vanguardist principles as articulated in the avant-garde journal *ABC* in 1925: "In modern design, deliberate, conscious organization supersedes the role of natural adaptation.... Modern art will consciously help itself to elements taken from nature.... The creation is governed by two directions of movement, the vertical and the horizontal.... Vertical and horizontal give architecture the right angle, which will constantly dominate the structure."[6]

Pohlenz's garden thus represented more of a rational construction than the romantic, naturalistic designs for numerous other contemporary gardens by professional landscape architects. The shaping elements were cubic forms and colors. Plants appeared no longer as individual trees, shrubs, and flowers, but exclusively as cubes and other space-creating forms. Pohlenz's garden unmistakably reflected the same creative principles as works of contemporary modern architecture, such as those by members of the Dutch De Stijl group like Theo van Doesburg and Cornelius van Eesteren, or the Schröder House in Utrecht by Gerrit Thomas Rietfeld.

Some of the works entered in the 1925 Juryfreie Kunstschau Berlin were discussed the following year

Queens Museum of Art
Down the Garden Path

Chapter 3
Essays

Fig. 1 (left) Hans Friedrich
Pohlenz, sketch for *Sonderbare
Garten* (Peculiar Garden), 1925.
From *Die Gartenkunst* 39, no. 6
(March 1926).

Fig. 2 (right) Gustav Allinger,
Auf dem Kristallberge (On Top of
Crystal Mountain), 1924. Allinger
showed this unrealized design
in 1924 at an exhibition of the
Verein Deutscher Gartenkünstler
in Bamberg. From *Die Gartenkunst*
37, no. 5 (1924).

{119}

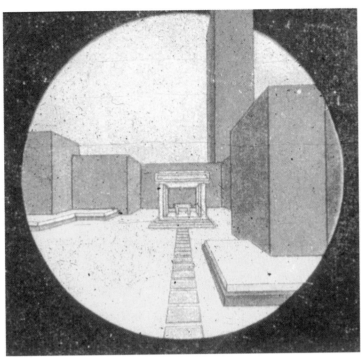

in *Die Gartenkunst* magazine. The reviewer, Fritz Wilhelm Schönfeld, made clear the difficulties that he had with the *Sonderbare Garten*, and revealed a markedly ambivalent attitude to Pohlenz's design. He did not dismiss modern art per se, but set Pohlenz's work in a negative context by completely unjustifiably comparing it with garden architect Gustav Allinger's 1924 Expressionistic experiment with a "*Kristallberg*" (Crystal Mountain; fig. 2). Schönfeld on Pohlenz: "When, in his work the '*Sonderbare Garten*,' he forms part of the earth in such a way that not many people can recognize the form as emerging from the organic, then we must attempt to get to the bottom of this idea. The Expressionist period, nowadays regarded by many as behind us, has undoubtedly encouraged parallel creations to this garden. I assume that Allinger's '*Kristallberg*,' with all its graphic failings, is really intended as no more than a lyrical paper bagatelle by an indubitably sure real creator. It is right and proper to dismiss the slogans of Expressionism."[7]

In conclusion, however, Schönfeld praises the "dignified impression" made by Pohlenz's *Sonderbare Garten*, recognizing it as a contribution to the quest for a garden that would coexist with the architecture of the *Neues Bauen* movement:

> It is clear to me that there may not be any slackening in the attempt to give the Gropiushaus (i.e., the Bauhaus movement) a garden of its own to which it is fundamentally attuned. On the other hand, this garden suits this house and no other. It is a garden for those who love the Gropiushaus, and it gives these owners an idea of how they and their successors could bring a garden for this house to fulfillment. For this reason I do not brand this garden a degenerate

child of the times, times in which many a soulless, irresponsible, and bizarre creation is claimed as evidence of a new spirit.[8]

This last remark of Schönfeld is harbinger of the diatribes of the National Socialist era, when many critics disqualified certain art as "degenerate" and their critiques contributed to the destruction of works of art and the defamation and professional and social isolation of their creators.

A further example that would indicate Pohlenz's familiarity with avant-garde design principles is his design for the *Wasserscheiben-Brunnen* (Water-Disk Fountain) shown in *Die Gartenschönheit* magazine in 1927 (fig. 3). Here, too, one finds the same playing with geometrical forms. A 1924 sculpture by George Vantongerloo (fig. 4), and Walter Dexel's 1920 *Farbige Lichtsäule II* (Colored-Light Column II; fig. 5), show astonishing affinities with Pohlenz's use of cubic forms and indicate that he was closely associated with these avant-garde design trends.

As a model, Pohlenz had taken an old fountain in Meersburg on the Bodensee and translated it into a modern language of form. He described his design intentions as follows: "In Meersburg on the Bodensee there stands an old fountain; a female figure holds her arms outstretched at head height, and a sheet of water plays between her hands. The jets spring from her palms. I have used this motif, divested of its romanticism, in a fountain for the Bergisches Land."[9]

To strip garden design of romanticism was the avant-garde credo, and one of the main motives of a small group of garden designers in Germany that included Heinz Wichmann, a landscape architect whose significance for avant-garde trends in

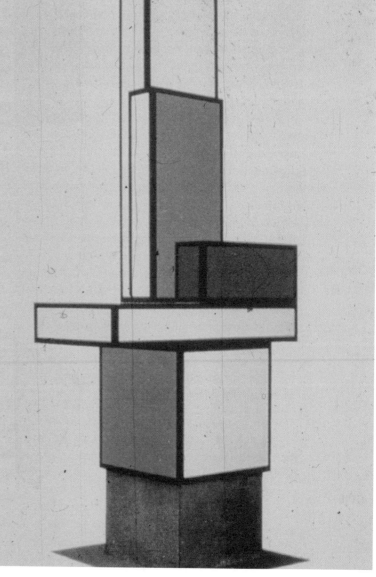

Queens Museum of Art
Down the Garden Path

Chapter 3
Essays

Fig. 3 (opposite page, top)
Hans Friedrich Pohlenz, sketch
for a *Wasserscheiben-Brunnen*
(Water-Disk Fountain). From
Die Gartenschönheit 8, no. 6
(June 1927).

Fig. 4 (opposite page, bottom
left) George Vantongerloo,
concrete sculpture, 1924. From
ABC, no. 2 (1926).

Fig. 5 (opposite page, bottom
right) Walter Dexel, *Farbige
Lichtsäule II* (Colored-Light

Column II), 1920. Reprinted in
Lufthansa Bordbuch, no. 1 (1992).

Fig. 6 (this page, left)
Heinz Wichmann, design for
a *Heidegarten*. From *Die
Gartenschönheit* 5, no. 9
(September 1924).

Fig. 7 (this page, right)
Traditional *Heidegarten*,
designed by the Späth firm,
Berlin, 1930s. From *Die
Gartenschönheit* 17, no. 4
(1936).

{121}

German garden design has long been overlooked. Wichmann, as has been discussed by Ulrich Müller, was affiliated with the Bauhaus in Weimar. In 1924 he wrote a memorandum in which he suggested establishing a garden-design class at the Bauhaus. Leading representatives of the Bauhaus such as Walter Gropius, Wassily Kandinsky, Paul Klee, and Oskar Schlemmer welcomed Wichmann's proposal, which, however, could not be implemented.[10]

In 1924 Wichmann described his design for a garden for a private house thus: "The garden presented here is an attempt to build a true house-garden—a garden as extension of the house, that one builds like the house, and that has grown organically with the house."[11] Wichmann's explanatory notes to the *Heidegarten* (heath garden; fig. 6), one of the garden spaces in this design, clarify his antiromanticist approach as set against traditional garden design, in that he expressly distances himself from the romanticist attitude to heath-garden designs: "An abstract sculpture in the little garden ensures that the picture is not comparable to that of a sentimental interpretation of the heath-garden idea."[12] A *Heidegarten* designed by the Späth firm in the 1930s (fig. 7) may elucidate the differences between an avant-garde and a romantic interpretation of this garden motif.

Avant-garde garden designers juxtaposed the organic forms of gardens—which they criticized as romantic, with their often-abundant vegetation arranged in a picturesque way—with gardens designed in a formal, functional way. They avoided organic forms and arrangements of plants that could be interpreted as natural and intended to evoke sentimental feelings. Such efforts to divest

garden design of romanticism, to offer a critique of sentimental heath gardens and to juxtapose them with other interpretations of the heath-garden idea were, in the heyday of the *Heideromantik* pastoral movement in literature and landscape painting, certainly avant-garde. The political resonance of garden-design statements by Wichmann, Pohlenz, and others should not be overinterpreted, but could in my estimation be understood as an attempt to deliberately address the conservative and reactionary political tendencies in garden architecture by artistic means. In the National Socialist era, only traditionalist ideas of gardens would prevail.

A 1927 design by landscape architect Heinrich Schmitz for a philosopher's garden can also be placed in this category (fig. 8). Schmitz described the brief from his client as follows: "Strictly ordered into the farthest corner, it was to be no ordinary domestic garden with all its little features. Soft contours were hated by the client; the lines thus are hard and severe. Despite this, the impression created by the entire grounds is ameliorated by the plantings, as the drawing technique indicates."[13] A similar interpretation of modern garden design to that of Pohlenz can be seen: Plants are no longer recognizable as single trees, shrubs, or flowers but essentially as masses and cubes defining space.

In France, avant-garde artists appear to have addressed the garden theme more intensively.[14] This can be deduced, for example, from the show gardens of Gabriel Guevrekian and the concrete trees of Mallet Stevens. And a garden planned by French architect André Lurcat (fig. 9) is remarkable less for its design than for the reactions it provoked in Germany, which shed light on the antimodernist trends within garden architecture in Germany that paved the way for the adoption of National Socialist dogma by the profession.

The characteristic quality of the Lurcat garden is a formal layout, its axial division by a watercourse and paths. The garden was presented to the German readership of *Gartenschönheit* magazine in 1930. Shortly after the article appeared, landscape architect Wilhelm Hübotter published his critique of Lurcat's garden in the form of a naturalist counterdesign in *Gartenkunst* magazine (fig. 10). The response to Lurcat's garden may thus be seen as marking the beginning of the eradication a little later under National Socialism of all avant-garde tendencies in German garden design.

In Germany, apparently, the work of avant-garde French architects and landscape architects was seen by conservative landscapers as even more provocative than comparable designs by their compatriot colleagues. Landscape architect Otto Valentien passed the following judgment on the Lurcat garden and a garden by Le Corbusier: "The consequences of both design principles remain alien to us; the result is an 'un-garden,' or rather, either a piece of decoration or a formless assortment of plants and paths."[15] Differing aesthetic ideas on the design of gardens can, of course, always be found, but to describe a garden as an "un-garden," as Valentien did Le Corbusier's and Lurcat's, signifies in the final analysis a dismissal of these representatives of modern trends in garden architecture that goes beyond discussion of content.

Two years earlier, in 1928, Alwin Seifert had, similarly to Valentien, emphatically criticized avant-garde French garden design in his "critical garden observations" on the Weißenhof housing settlement in Stuttgart. After 1933 Seifert, a fanatic anti-Semite, became one of the leading Nazi garden architects. In his 1928 article he compared avant-garde French garden design negatively with the modern trends in Germany: "Even so, all this is better than what is nowadays being created in Romanesque countries. One must come from France, where today still in public grounds the beds are enclosed in tree trunks of cast concrete, to adopt a position like Le Corbusier as the only one of the Weißenhof architects to have created the garden himself."[16]

The critique by Hübotter of the Lurcat garden, in the form of a counterdesign, and the written critiques by Valentien and Seifert of modern design movements in France illustrate the ideological shift that was emerging in Germany towards the end of the Weimar Republic and which helped the one-sided dissemination of ideas of garden design "rooted in the soil"—of the use of putatively indigenous plants and building materials—to attain dominance. Many garden architects were not prepared to tolerate avant-garde and other design experiments and defamed them as degenerate, un-German, or un-gardenlike.

The aesthetic, functional, and other qualities of these experiments are, at this juncture, of secondary importance. Some could have offered stimuli for future garden designs, but ultimately the ideas on garden design as developed by Pohlenz, Pniower, Wichmann, and others were disqualified and their systematic development brought to a halt. That with which they were confronted, by Hübotter, Seifert, Valentien, and their ilk, was in its function and aesthetics not without its qualities. The dictatorship of taste as exercised a little later under the conditions created by the Nazi state, however, brought about a limitation to these and other design trends and principles.

The End of Experimentation in the Garden Arts

Transfer of power to the National Socialists in January 1933 put an end, also in garden architecture, to the lively experiments of the Weimar period.[17] To the creative disciplines, the Nazi dictatorship meant not only the expulsion of "inconvenient" people from state office and the freelance professions and the "consolidation" of professional organizations but also an onslaught on experimental forms of artistic expression. The Bauhaus was closed down. Numerous progressive artists and intellectuals left the country. The *"Entartete Kunst"* (Degenerate Art) exhibition of 1937 singled out the Expressionists for particular defamation.[18]

In garden architecture there were equally vituperative attacks on the reform attempts of the 1920s. Numerous publications between 1933 and 1945 were little more than a categorical settling of scores with efforts during the Weimar Republic to introduce artistic innovations in garden architecture. In 1936 the dendrologist Camillo Schneider, for example, fulminated against Expressionism as irreconcilable with the fundamental idea of the garden: "When the mighty reorientation arrived, nowhere did it find the soil better prepared for its ideas than in gardening and garden design. More and more exertions were made to apprehend the living habitat of the garden, to reiterate the bond of 'blood and soil.' The garden as a living organism attuned to the rules of nature cannot sustain Expressionism, derived as it is from dry, intellectualized reason."[19] Josef Pertl, for many years a member of the Nazi Party (NSDAP) and director of gardens in Berlin from 1935, ranted in 1937: "When zigzag became modern in postwar architecture, people made zigzags in garden design as well. The term 'modern' has also been prevalent in garden design, and there must be an end to these times once and for

Queens Museum of Art
Down the Garden Path

Chapter 3
Essays

Fig. 8 (top) Heinrich Schmitz, design for a modernist garden for a philosopher. From *Die Gartenschönheit* 8, no. 8 (August 1927).

Fig. 9 (bottom left) Garden of André Lurcat, France. From *Die Gartenschönheit* 9, no. 5 (1930).

Fig. 10 (bottom right) Plan for the Lurcat Garden (top left); counterdesign by Wilhelm Hübotter (top right); and sketch of the Hübotter garden (bottom). From *Die Gartenkunst* 43, no. 7 (1930).

{123}

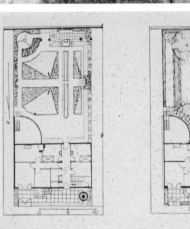

all."[20] With such words Pertl dragged designs such as that for the Garten Buchthal by Eryk Pepinski into the area of "*entartete Kunst*" to endanger the occupations and the very lives of such garden architects.

Hans Hasler was another Nazi garden designer who vilified experimentation in the garden architecture of the 1920s. In his book *Deutsche Gartenkunst* he referred to a race-specific and national art: "All art, and thus all the arts and their styles are—this truth has constantly prevailed in Germany—always derived from national and racial origins and life. The illusion of an 'international' culture, a 'world culture,' is a thing of the past, at least for us as Germans."[21] His polemic against Expressionism asserted:

> This movement, diametrically opposed to Impressionism, is alien to healthy German sensibilities; it is the expression of the artistic activity of the Near Eastern-oriental peoples. Its protagonists contend that they thereby seek to express inner spiritual experiences and thus justify altering the depicted form.... Henceforth the new era has put an end to all this hocus-pocus.... German architecture is experiencing a Nordic revival through its best champions Speer, Todt, Troost, and others.... Willy Lange has initiated a parallel development with his works in word and deed.[22]

Hasler, a member of the NSDAP since April 1928, was well placed to propagate his ideas on garden design under National Socialism, in among other roles as head of the garden art section at the Geisenheim teaching and research center for viticulture, fruit growing, and horticulture. The Berlin garden designer F. C. Weigold, who was a member of an SA storm-trooper division before 1933 and later an NSDAP official, ranted in 1935 against the modernists in garden architecture: "The Jewish mindset, which ridicules everything typically German, is still embedded in their subconscious."[23]

Sketches and designs for gardens such as those of Pohlenz, Wichmann, and Pniower from the 1920s would have been defamed by Pertl, Hasler, Weigold, and others in the Nazi period as "degenerate" if they could have been published in professional journals at all. These few quotations can only give an indication of how under National Socialism artistic freedoms were restricted and dismantled in the private sphere of the garden as well.

For considerations of garden design in Germany, National Socialism signified a serious caesura that apparently had an influence on developments in the Federal Republic of Germany after 1945, particularly in the pernicious lack of innovation and paucity of discussion of provocative and stimulating ideas in garden architecture, and an artistic break that was to influence developments far into the era of the Federal Republic as well as the former German Democratic Republic. Landscape architect Georg Bela Pniower described the creation and destruction of avant-garde trends in German garden design in retrospect as professor of garden and landscape design at Humboldt University in East Berlin. Pniower

Queens Museum of Art
Down the Garden Path

Chapter 3
Essays

Fig. 11 (opposite page, left)
Georg Bela Pniower, interior
garden for the Gourmenia House,
Berlin, 1920s. From the Archives
Humboldt-Universität Berlin.

Fig. 12 (opposite page, right)
Georg Bela Pniower, *Kurven im
Garten Dr. Hoffmann* (Curves in
Dr. Hoffmann's Garden), 1920s.
From the Archives Humboldt-
Universität Berlin.

{125}

was one of the most progressive landscape architects in twentieth-century Germany. During the
Weimar period he developed innovative concepts for
garden design (figs. 11 and 12). Under National
Socialism he was persecuted by the state as a member of the Social Democratic Party and as a person of
"half-Jewish" origin, and excluded from the profession by *Berufsverbot* until 1945. After liberation
from National Socialism, he became chairholder for
garden and landscape design at Humboldt University.

Pniower described in the 1950s the rise and
destruction of avant-garde garden design in moving terms:

> In the period between the two wars, all over the world
> creative forces were moving. That led, after the hor-
> rors of the *Gründerzeit* [period of German hegemo-
> nization] and after the woolliness of the times before
> the wars, to a new development in style. This dawn
> had already left distinct and guiding marks in the
> arts. Almost at the same time there developed, on
> different continents and among different peoples,
> the same endeavors. These promising revolutionary
> forces—slandered by the petty-bourgeois as degen-
> erate—were stopped when Hitler started his cam-
> paign against culture and humankind. As First
> Master Builder of the Reich, as he styled himself, he
> referred to the ancient Teutons, caused every petty-
> bourgeois heart to beat faster when he had his
> *Kulturkammer* [Reich Chamber for Cultural Affairs]
> announce the new Renaissance, and finally went so
> far as to appeal to Goethe, Mozart, Balthasar
> Neumann, the *Bauhütten*, etc.—even to the ancient
> Greeks—as witnesses of the grandeur of his ideas
> about culture. Our beautiful, venerable architectural
> monuments, which no modern architect of the
> *Systemzeit* [period of the Weimar Republic] would
> have dared touch; each farmer's garden that would
> gladden the heart of even the most decadent urban-
> ite; each piece of untouched landscape that the city
> dweller appreciated on his travels and in his love of
> nature were suddenly called as witnesses to prove
> that everything modern, everything questing, every
> experiment on the path to a new and up-to-date
> design of our environment was barbarism, deca-
> dence, degeneration; in a word, of Jewish spirit.[24]

The Garden as a Place of Refuge in the National Socialist Period

Under National Socialism the private garden
could—at least for a while—be especially important
as a place where people could move relatively freely,
away from Nazi checks, without having to wear the
Star of David or submit to other restrictions. Herta
Hammerbacher, an important twentieth-century
German garden architect, once described garden

architecture during National Socialism as "inner
emigration." Even when such a generalizing inclu-
sion of a period's entire garden architecture with a
single term cannot be sustained, such a typification
may be valid for the importance of the private garden to numerous people persecuted by the Nazis—
the garden as a place of "inner emigration," of
Mattern's "freedom within limits." The garden probably had an especially heightened significance for
thousands of Jewish citizens who through the
1930s were subjected to increasing repression,
exclusion, and persecution.[25]

Today we have a large number of research projects that vividly portray and interpret the Nazi
reign of terror and show how crucially important
under such circumstances—defamation, restrictions on freedom of movement, destruction of the
private sphere (through, e.g., the compulsory wearing of the Star of David)—was a garden of one's
own in which, temporarily, one could move without
hindrance. A companion volume to an exhibition
on Jewish life in Berlin from 1938 to 1945 stated:
"The Nazi terror increasingly intruded on the
details of everyday life. Admission to parks, public
houses, woods, railway stations, and restricted
areas was prohibited. . . . Jews were not allowed to
use public transport and ticket machines. They
were forbidden to keep pets."[26]

The significance of the garden as a refuge and one
of the last remaining places of private—if limited—
freedom is vividly described in the diaries of writer
and academic Victor Klemperer. In the entry for
May 23, 1938, he wrote of his wife, "Eva bull-headed
as ever—still planting, planning, hoping."[27] And on
June 20, 1939: "The garden is in bloom as never
before: roses, roses, jasmine, carnations, helianthe-
mum."[28] It seems almost as if Klemperer is juxtaposing the "blooming" of the Nazi dictatorship with the
blooms in his own garden.

During several days in prison in June 1941,
Klemperer looked back on the importance of the
house and garden to his wife: "And when you, ever
more passionately, sought to compensate for the
music as it slipped away, as it became more difficult
to get around, as the garden, our own house, became
the be-all and end-all, how long I resisted, how
late—almost too late—acceded."[29] For other fellow-
sufferers, too, Klemperer's diary entries reveal the
importance of the garden. On November 9, 1941,
he wrote: "Since September 19, the day on which
wearing the Star of David became compulsory,
Kreidl senior and Dr. Friedheim have not left the
house. With Friedheim it's of his own will, with Kreidl
probably the will of his Aryan wife who doesn't want
to be compromised. When the weather's fine, both
men work in the garden, and they've been shut in for

a while now. They must be going crazy, and one senses their agitation."[30]

As another prominent example, reference may be made to the Berlin publisher Julius Springer, who during the Nazi period retreated increasingly into his garden and, after the wearing of the Star of David was made compulsory, never left his house and garden again.[31]

Nevertheless, the Nazi encroachments eventually reached the gardens and other residential spaces of the Jewish population. For example, in the Tiergarten district of Berlin in autumn 1934, "action was taken against the building of sukkah [structures that commemorate the temporary shelters of the Jews during their wandering in the wilderness] in courtyards and on balconies on the pretext of building regulations."[32] In September 1939 there followed an order prohibiting the erection of sukkah in synagogues for the annual Feast of Tabernacles, and individuals were also forbidden to set up sukkah.[33]

In his entry for December 9, 1939, Klemperer wrote of the blow that had long been expected—notice to quit their house by April and thus to give up their garden: "Eva more composed than I, although she is more affected: *her* house, *her* garden, *her* occupation. For her it will be as if in prison."[34] This entry especially, with its reference to imprisonment, is an obvious reference to the immense significance that the garden probably held as a place of "freedom within limits" for many who were persecuted under National Socialism for their religion, descent, or political convictions. In the light of the value placed on the garden, these further repressive measures of the NS state recorded by Klemperer must be regarded as even more serious: the "dejewification" of property and ejection of Jewish families from their homes and thus from their gardens.

Disenfranchisement of the Jewish population and extensive intrusions into the private sphere began after the National Socialists came to power in 1933. This is reflected in numerous laws and regulations, among them the *Reichsbürgergesetz* (Reich Citizenship Law) of September 15, 1935; the *Gesetz zum Schutze des deutschen Blutes und der deutschen Ehre* (Law for the Protection of German Blood and Honor) of the same date; and the *Verordnung über die Anmeldung des Vermögens von Juden* (Ordinance on the Registration of Jewish Property) of April 26, 1938.[35] On December 3, 1938, shortly after November 9's *Kristallnacht*, an ordinance on the assignment of Jewish property (*Verordnung über den Einsatz des jüdischen Vermögens*) was passed that included real estate.[36] These and other ordinances made it possible to deprive the Jewish population of its houses and lands. The study *Juden in Berlin 1938-1945* con-

tains a striking account of this "dejewification of living space" and the subsequent establishment of *Judenhäuser* (Jew houses).[37]

After being driven from their house and garden and moving into the Judenhaus at Caspar-David-Friedrich-Straße 15b, the Klemperers no longer had their own garden, only a balcony—but even this seems to have been important as "free space." The balcony is repeatedly mentioned in Klemperer's diary entries, for example on May 26, 1940: "A pretty villa, built too narrow, too 'modern,' packed with people sharing the same fate. Beautifully located in the countryside. Old parkland divided into properties, behind the rows of trees and gardens, meadows and arable land; when we stand on the balcony away from the street, to the right the view is limited by a pebbledash wall, to the left by a clinic.... Everything in full bloom, lilac, chestnut, spring in all its forms. Glorious gardens along the wide Waterloostrasse.... All in all, Dresden at its most beautiful."[38]

Various investigations of political resistance to the Nazi dictatorship show that private areas—above all, house, apartment, and garden—assumed importance not only as places of "freedom within limits," of retreat into the private sphere, but also as places of resistance, conspiratorial meetings, and hiding from Nazi persecution. The weekend gardens and *Kleingärten* (allotment gardens) especially must be included in this picture. One investigation states: "The private sphere—the apartment, one's fellow tenants in the house and the neighborhood—is where most illegal activities took place.... The private sphere was not only more out of the reach of the persecuting authorities than the public and semipublic context, but also offered a variety of opportunities for communication beyond those of neighborly contacts."[39]

Above all with regard to allotment gardens and garden sheds, there are many references to confirm that they served persecuted Jews and other persons pursued for political reasons as hiding places and bases for resistance. According to garden architect Herta Hammerbacher, her colleague Georg Bela Pniower, banned from practicing his profession, went into hiding in allotment gardens in Berlin.[40] Taking the Berlin allotment-garden colonies as an example, their significance under National Socialism is comprehensively documented in the study *Ein starkes Stück Berlin. 1901-2001. 100 Jahre organisiertes Kleingartenwesen in Berlin.*[41] The series of publications by the Gedenkstätte Deutscher Widerstand (Memorial Institute for German Resistance) entitled *Widerstand 1933-1945 Berlin*, which documents the resistance in Berlin with examples from the city districts, also bears repeated witness to the importance of allotment-garden colonies as refuges for persecuted Jews and victims of political persecution and as places that served to support victims of the Nazi regime by other means.

A particularly vivid example of the importance of the allotment garden as refuge is found in the auto-biography of television show host Hans Rosenthal, *Zwei Leben in Deutschland* (Two Lives in Germany). As a youth Rosenthal was persecuted for his Jewish descent and in 1943 sought refuge with a family acquaintance who hid him for almost two years in a small room of her garden cottage in the Berlin-Lichtenberg allotment colony Dreieinigkeit. Rosenthal describes his situation in the allotment gardens vividly; the view from his little hiding place into a tiny garden space meant a great deal to him in his situation: "When I looked through my skylight window, the view was limited: six square meters of lawn, a wire fence surrounding Frau Jauch's little chicken run, behind it a hedge and over the hedge a tree. That was all . . . but what a consolation during my nerve-wracking imprisonment."[42]

The night bombing raids by the British that brought fear and horror to most Berliners gave Rosenthal the freedom to emerge from his hiding place and enjoy the garden and nature. "The best time for me was when the air-raid sirens sounded at night and the 'enemy' airplanes came," he writes. "Then other people went to the bunkers, and I could come out of the cottage. Then, while others higher up the pecking order were trembling in the bunkers—God knows, I didn't envy them—I felt safe. When the sirens went off, with their ululating screams warning of an air raid, my heart beat faster. As soon as the others had disappeared into the bunkers I ran, I stormed out of the cottage. I recognized the aircraft-engine noises and also knew at about what height they flew over. In the summer I lay down on the grass, folded my arms behind my head and looked up into the Berlin night sky. Then, life was almost beautiful. For me, the English were 'responsible'—they came at night. During the day the Americans came. They were no use to me, as I didn't dare emerge in daylight."[43]

The autobiographical account of the actor Michael Degen repeatedly makes clear the importance of allotment gardens and weekend cottages as tempo-rary hiding places for Jews on the run from the authorities. An acquaintance "put her cottage at [my] disposal without knowing for whom and for what pur-pose. Probably she didn't want to know at all."[44] How temporary such refuges often were and, in the case of gardens, how dependent on the seasons and thus planting and gardening times became clear when the acquaintance indicated that he could hide in the gar-den only until the beginning of spring: "When winter's past you'll have to be out of here, because then the gardeners will be back to set their bulbs."[45]

During the Second World War gardens acquired a further importance for people threatened by the Nazi reign of terror. When the Jewish population was excluded from the protection of air-raid bunkers, the many *Splittergräben* shelters in gardens offered occasional protection from bombs. This protective function of the garden is also described in Degen's autobiography: "After the cinema we strolled right through Tiergarten to the Brandenburg Gate. Mother thought we should take the tram to the suburbs, per-haps to Erkner or Straußberg, where if there was raid we could shelter in a *Splitterbunker*. *Splitterbunker* was the name for trenches that all garden owners had to dig when their house was too far away from a public bunker—a trench with a roof supported on wooden beams that anyone caught out in the open during an air raid had to be admitted to."[46]

The Instrumentalization of Public Gardens for the Persecution of Jews

To conclude, the issue of how public parks and gar-dens were used under National Socialism to discrimi-nate against and persecute the Jewish population should be addressed. Not only were they deprived of their private gardens; the use of public parks was made increasingly difficult and often completely prohibited.

In the course of National Socialist society, more and more local authorities passed bylaws to exclude Jews from parks and other public open spaces. In some cities, such as Hannover and Berlin, prohibitions seem to have begun very soon after the Nazis seized power. The records of the Hannover city council from 1933 provide plentiful evidence of efforts to exclude the Jewish population from public baths and sports facilities.[47] In Berlin, as early as August 1933, bathing was prohibited for Jews at the Wannsee lido. A decree of July 1935 by the Lord Mayor denied them admis-sion to all public baths and a notice was erected at Wannsee, "Bathing and Admission Prohibited for Jews," later removed at the request of the foreign ministry because of the Berlin Olympiad.[48] In Berlin such measures were also continually extended and made more severe in public open spaces. For exam-ple, in November 1937, yellow park benches were set up in Berliner Westen. Apparently, the gardens department of the Prenzlauer Berg had previously affixed notices to 92 of the 100 benches in the public gardens, "Use by Jews Prohibited." In a study of Jewish policy in the Third Reich, the marking of park benches as "For Germans Only" is shown to be one of the many measures used to humiliate and discriminate against the Jewish population that had become normal after 1938.[49] There are num-erous accounts from Jewish citizens affected by this measure.[50]

Victor Klemperer's diaries also offer a striking example of the banning of Jews from public gardens. In 1940 a Dresden city council bylaw prohibited the Jewish population from entering the Großer Garten, a ban whose significance Klemperer suggested on November 28, 1938, in a diary entry as follows: "The old major said to me, 'Between these four walls you can say what you think. These days I hear many shocking things, and I go for walks in my spare time in the Großer Garten to calm down.'"[51] On July 6, 1940, Klemperer wrote in his diary, "A new prohibition for Jews, on entering the Großer Garten and other parks. Effect on the Judenhaus." In connection with the recently passed exclusion order for the Großer Garten in Dresden, Klemperer emphasizes the uncertainty as particularly oppressive: "Nobody knows exactly what's permitted; one feels threatened wherever one goes. Every animal has more liberty and security under the law than we do."[52]

The Leipzig municipal administration also appears to have been very diligent in limiting opportunities for Jewish citizens to use the public parks. This is particularly clear from the example of Rosental, an important park for which garden artist Eduard Petzold had prepared reconstruction designs in the late 1870s.[53] A recent paper by Sylvia Kabus provides shocking examples of the suppression—with the active participation of individual citizens—of the Jewish population and their expulsion from Rosental as an important place for recreation (fig. 13):

> Located directly in the Waldstraßenviertel [district], [Rosental] was the park used most frequently by the many Jewish citizens of Leipzig that lived in the vicinity.... The files of the City of Leipzig central administration not only record the disenfranchisement of the Jews and the actions of the administration; they are also shocking in the zeal with which individuals, without instructions from above, acted against their fellow human beings and forced the pace of this dreadful procedure. The green spaces of Rosental became an object of oppressive squabbling about the very right of the Jews to be anywhere.[54]

Apparently the Leipzig municipal administration received many defamatory letters from citizens complaining about the presence of Jewish citizens in Rosental and their behavior there. A letter dated 1937 to Mayor Rudolf Haake:

> Everyone complains that most of the benches are occupied by the sons and daughters of Israel, that they are in no way disconcerted and do not vacate them when 'Aryans' wish to take a seat, and thus a suppressed battle flares up between them with the result that the shameless and thick-skinned *Itzigs* win.... Admittedly, the Jews are also taxpayers and Rosental is a public amenity, but it must not come to

such a pass that the Jews feel 'at home' there.... On fine summer days the Jews sit with their dependents in the café in Kleiner Garten basking in the sun. ... Would it not be possible to assign them to particular houses and thus create a ghetto, as was usual in the Middle Ages, where they could be among their own kind?[55]

Because of such complaints, in 1937 the Leipzig parks and gardens department made inquiries with the municipal administrations in Berlin, Breslau, Frankfurt am Main, Hamburg, Cologne, and Königsberg about their experience: "We have received suggestions from residents of the city to allot some ten percent of the benches to Jews in a woodland park much frequented by Jews. Before I respond to these suggestions I would be interested to hear whether you have had to address this issue and how the matter has been dealt with."[56] Until then other garden and city administrations had apparently not seen any necessity to take action. Discriminatory and oppressive measures against the Jewish population, both in public parks and other open spaces in Leipzig and other cities, were to increase enormously in 1938.

A precondition for the functioning of the Nazi dictatorship was, however, the voluntary support of numerous Germans. The consistent persecution of Jews in all areas of public and private life during National Socialism required the active and willing collaboration of many people who, for example, directed appropriate complaints to municipal administrations, to city garden departments, to the press and other institutions. The Leipzig example shows to what shocking lengths this could be taken, but other cities such as Bremen, Hannover, and Berlin also offer regrettable instances. There and in other cities, complaints from citizens can be found about the behavior or even the mere presence of Jewish citizens in swimming pools, parks, and other places that led to their prohibition and exclusion. Members of the Berlin municipal administration, particularly, appear to have assumed an active role in this matter. Gruner, in his study of the persecution of Jews in Berlin from 1933 to 1945, concluded, "Through this chronology there runs a clear indication of the assiduous and ingenious participation of the civic authorities in the suppression and exclusion of Jewish Berliners after 1933."[57]

In her study of the Jews of Bremen under National Socialism, Regina Bruss presents a striking picture of the dimensions of such persecutory measures:

> Sooner or later, whenever the question of regulating the appearance of Jews in the public domain arose, the use of public open spaces and gardens was at issue. This seems at first sight of no greater impor-

Queens Museum of Art
Down the Garden Path

Chapter 3
Essays

Fig. 13 Members of the Hitler
Youth in Park Rosental, Leipzig,
ca. 1939. Reprinted in Sylvia
Kabus, "Zwischen Rose und
Lindenbaum," *Leipziger Blätter*,
no. 42 (2003).

{129}

Hitlerjungen auf dem Weg zum HJ-Heim oder zur Jugendherberge im Rosental – ihre jüdischen Altersgenossen und deren Familien sollen sich hier nicht erholen dürfen.

tance, but on closer consideration it becomes clear what it means, for instance, never to be able to sit down on a bench without others shifting along or standing up. While elsewhere those responsible were wrestling with regulations on "the use of benches in public parks and amenities" [according to the German council of local authorities' news agency on November 1, 1937, some cities were considering, "to remove the cause of some deplorable events, allotting only a certain number of benches in parks and public amenities for the use of Jews"; quoted in Bruss, 133], Bremen had no need to think of a solution, as [according to a November 16 communication from the gardens and cemeteries department] "the Jews here are unobtrusive and hardly ever seen in the public gardens."[58]

It is remarkable that until now little light has been shed on this shocking chapter of the recent history of the culture of gardens in Germany. To the best of my knowledge, none of the innumerable works on the history of any historic garden—be it the Großer Garten in Dresden, the Bremen Wallanlagen, the Großer Garten in Herrenhausen, or any other—has addressed the issue that under National Socialism the Jewish population was denied access to many public parks and gardens, while garden historians studying the Nazi era return time and again to lamenting the widespread destruction that Allied air raids caused to such historic grounds during the Second World War.[59] These aspects, the instrumentalization of the parks in persecuting the Jews, and the importance of private gardens as (temporary) refuges in the Nazi era all require more intense research; at present we have only a few pieces of the mosaic.

Acknowledgments
This essay is a revised version of a paper that was published in 2003 in Siegfried Lamnek and Marie-Theres Tinnefeld, eds., *Privatheit, Garten und politische Kultur. Von kommunikativen Zwischenräumen* (Opladen, Germany: Leske + Buderich, 2003), 155–84. Sections of the first part of the paper on modern trends in early-twentieth-century garden design in Germany have been published under the title "The Avant-garde and garden architecture in Germany: On a forgotten phenomenon of the Weimar period" in *Centropa: A Journal of Central European Architecture and Related Arts* 4, no. 2 (2004): 100–111. I am grateful to Tinnefeld and Lamnek, and to Dora Wiebenson, the editor of *Centropa*, for giving permission to use those contributions for this article.

I would like to thank Mic Hale for his excellent and sensitive translation and for continuing a fruitful collaboration.

NOTES

1 For biographies of Hermann Mattern and other landscape architects mentioned in this paper, see Gert Gröning and Joachim Wolschke-Bulmahn, *Grüne Biographie. Biographisches Handbuch der Landschaftsarchitektur des 20. Jahrhunderts in Deutschland* (Berlin and Hannover: Patzer Verlag, 1997).

2 Mention should be made here of another publication with the same title. It was published in 1993 by Edith Dietz, a Jew who was able to escape from Nazi persecution into Switzerland in 1942 and who, in the volume *Freiheit in Grenzen* (Frankfurt: dipa-Verlag, 1993), recounts her experiences between 1942 and her return to Germany in 1946.

3 The text of Mattern's brochure, however, offers no indication that the title could be construed as a subtle criticism of National Socialism.

4 See in more detail, e.g., Joachim Wolschke-Bulmahn and Gert Gröning, "'Der kommende Garten.' Zur Diskussion über die Gartenarchitektur in Deutschland seit 1900," *Garten und Landschaft* 98, no. 3 (1988): 47–56; Gert Gröning and Joachim Wolschke-Bulmahn, "Changes in the philosophy of garden architecture in the 20th century and their impact upon the social and spatial environment," *Journal of Garden History* 9, no. 2 (1988): 53–70; Uwe Schneider, "Hermann Muthesius und die Reformdiskussion in der Gartenarchitektur des frühen 20. Jahrhunderts," *Grüne Reihe—Quellen und Forschungen zur Gartenkunst*, vol. 21 (Worms: Wernersche Verlagsgesellschaft, 2000).

5 The following passages on the *Sonderbare Garten* and avant-garde garden design in Germany are taken from Joachim Wolschke-Bulmahn, "The Avant-garde and garden architecture in Germany: On a forgotten phenomenon of the Weimar period," *Centropa* 4, no. 2 (2004): 100–111.

6 "Modernes Bauen 2," *ABC*, no. 3/4 (1925): n. p.

7 Fritz Wilhelm Schönfeld, "Kritische Betrachtungen über drei Hausgärten (Pohlenz—Hübotter—Valentien)," *Die Gartenkunst* 39, no. 3 (March 1926): 36.

8 Ibid., 42.

9 Hans Friedrich Pohlenz, "Ein Wasserscheiben-Brunnen," *Die Gartenschönheit* 8, no. 6 (June 1927): 159.

10 Ulrich Müller, "Der Garten des Hauses Auerbach," *Die Gartenkunst* 11, no. 1 (1999): 109.

11 Heinz Wichmann, "Ein Wohngarten," *Die Gartenschönheit* 5, no. 9 (September 1924): 169.

12 Ibid., 171.

13 Heinrich Schmitz, "Haus und Garten," *Die Gartenschönheit* 8, no. 8 (August 1927): 215.

14 See in connection with this subject Dorothee Imbert, *The Modernist Garden in France* (New Haven, CT, and London: Yale University Press, 1993).

15 Otto Valentien, "Neuzeitliche Gartengestaltung," *Die Gartenkunst* 43, no. 7 (1930): 104.

16 Alwin Seifert, "Die Stuttgarter Weißenhof-Siedlung in gartenkritischer Betrachtung," *Die Gartenkunst* 41, no. 4 (1928): 59.

17 See also Gert Gröning and Joachim Wolschke-Bulmahn, "Zur Entwicklung und Unterdrückung freiraumplanerischer Ansätze der Weimarer Republik," *Das Gartenamt* 34, no. 6 (1985): 443–57.

18 Regarding Expressionism and garden design in Germany, see in more detail Peter Fibich and Joachim Wolschke-Bulmahn, "'Gartenexpressionismus.' Anmerkungen zu einer historischen Debatte," *Stadt und Grün* 53, no. 8 (2004): 27–34.

19 Camillo Schneider, "Was lehrt Dresden den Gartenfreund? Kritische Anmerkungen für eine künftige Reichsgartenschau," *Die Gartenschönheit* 17, no. 9 (1936): 196.

20 Josef Pertl, "Weltanschauung und Gartenkunst, anlässlich der Jubiläumstagung in Düsseldorf am 4. Juli 1937," *Die Gartenkunst* 50, no. 10 (1937): 215.

21 Hans Hasler, *Deutsche Gartenkunst. Entwicklung, Form und Inhalt des deutschen Gartens* (Stuttgart: Ulmer-Verlag, 1939), 15.

22 Ibid., 22ff.

23 F[riedrich] C[ornelius] Weigold, "Romantik im Garten," *Die Gartenkunst* 48, no. 4 (1935): 67.

24 Georg Bela Pniower, draft for a lecture on landscape design, n.d., Ka4, Ma8, Humboldt University Archive, Berlin. I thank Peter Fibich for drawing my attention to this manuscript. Regarding Pniower in more detail, see Joachim Wolschke-Bulmahn and Peter Fibich, *Vom Sonnerenrund zur Beispiellandschaft. Entwicklungslinien der Landschaftsarchitektur in Deutschland, dargestellt am Werk von Georg Pniower (1896-1960)*, Beiträge zur räumlichen Planung, vol. 73 (Hannover: University of Hannover Department of Landscape Architecture, 2004).

25 On the role of the garden in this connection there is still a great need for research. When, as recently as 1996, an expert in research on anti-Semitism in the city of Berlin can still say, "Till today, little is known about the lives of Berlin Jews under Nazi persecution," it is to be expected that there are probably no research findings whatsoever on the role that gardens played in the lives of the Jewish population at that time. (Wolf Gruner, *Judenverfolgung in Berlin 1933-1945. Eine Chronologie der Behördenmaßnahmen in der Reichshauptstadt*, Stiftung Topographie des Terrors [Berlin: Edition Hertrich, 1996], 6.)

26 Beate Meyer and Hermann Simon, eds., *Juden in Berlin 1938-1945* (Berlin: Philo Verlagsgesellschaft mbH, 2000), 99. Companion volume to an exhibition at the Neue Synagoge Berlin—Centrum Judaicum, May–August 2000.

27 Victor Klemperer, *Ich will Zeugnis ablegen bis zum letzten: Tagebücher 1933-1941*, vol. 1 (Berlin: Aufbau-Verlag, 1995; 11th printing, 1999), 409.

28 Ibid., 474.

29 Ibid., 635.

30 Ibid., 685.

31 Verbal communication by the granddaughter of Julius Springer to Wolfgang Immenhausen, n.d.

32 Gruner, *Judenverfolgung*, 33.

33 Ibid., 69.

34 Klemperer, *Tagebücher*, 503.

35 For a full account of National Socialist legislation, see *Gesetze des NS-Staates. Dokumente eines Unrechtsystems*, compiled and with an introduction by Uwe Brodersen, published by Ingo von Münch (Paderborn,

Munich, Vienna, and Zurich: Ferdinand Schöningh, 1968; 2nd edition, 1982). See also Kai Henning and Josef Kestler, "Die Rechtsstellung der Juden, " in E.-W. Bockenförde, ed., *Staatsrecht und Staatsrechtslehre im Dritten Reich* (Heidelberg: C. F. Müller Juristischer Verlag, 1985), 191–211.

36 Regina Bruss, *Die Bremer Juden unter dem National-sozialismus*, from the archives of the Hanseatic City of Bremen, vol. 49, published by Wilhelm Lührs (Bremen: Staatsarchivs der Freien Hansestadt Bremen, 1983), 113.

37 Meyer and Simon, *Juden in Berlin*, 97.

38 Klemperer, *Tagebücher*, 527–28. Entries for June 11, 1940: "In the mornings Frau Voß comes into our bedroom and onto the adjoining balcony" (534); and June 29, 1940: "We have bought a flower trough for the balcony and a few flowerpots" (535).

39 Hans-Dieter Schmid, "Zur Sozialstruktur des organisierten Widerstands der Arbeiterschaft in Hannover," in Frank Bajohr, ed., *Norddeutschland im National-sozialismus*, Forum Zeitgeschichte, vol. 1, published by the Forschungsstelle für die Geschichte des Nationalsozialismus in Hamburg (Hamburg: Ergebnisse-Verlag, 1993), 139.

40 Herta Hammerbacher, "Eine Entgegnung," *Bauwelt* 68, no. 28 (1977): 964.

41 *Ein starkes Stück Berlin. 1901–2001. 100 Jahre organisiertes Kleingartenwesen in Berlin*, ed. Landesverband Berlin der Gartenfreunde e.V. (Berlin: Verlag W. Wächter GmbH., 2001), 142ff.

42 Hans Rosenthal, *Zwei Leben in Deutschland* (Bergisch-Gladbach, Germany: Gustav Lübbe Verlag, 1980), 62ff. For the importance of allotment gardens for Rosenthal and the situation in the night air raids, see also Michael Schäbitz, "'Wir waren Ausgestoßene im eigenen Vaterland.' Überleben in der NS-Zeit, Das Beispiel Hans Rosenthal," in Meyer and Simon, *Juden in Berlin*, 284–85; see, similarly, *Ein starkes Stück Berlin*, 142ff.

43 Rosenthal, *Zwei Leben*, 64.

44 Michael Degen, *Nicht alle waren Mörder: Eine Kindheit in Berlin* (Munich: Ullstein-Verlag, 2003), 83.

45 Ibid., 116.

46 Ibid., 34.

47 Revealed by research by Dr. Peter Schulze of the Hannover City Archives.

48 Gruner, *Judenverfolgung in Berlin*, 29ff.

49 Uwe Dietrich Adam, *Judenpolitik im Dritten Reich*, Tübinger Schriften zur Sozial- und Zeitgeschichte, vol. 1, published by Gerhard Schulz (Düsseldorf: Droste Verlag, 1972), 194.

50 See, e.g., the account of Irmgard Amith, whose family was compelled in 1938 to sell its house in Düsseldorf and who relates that from that year she was no longer permitted to sit on the benches in the park in Düsseldorf (it is unclear whether she meant all parks in Düsseldorf or a particular park in her neighborhood). See Hans-Peter Görgen, *Dokumentation zur Geschichte der Stadt Düsseldorf im "Dritten Reich" 1935-1945: Quellensammlung* (Düsseldorf: Pädagogisches Institut der Landeshauptstadt Düsseldorf, 1983), 281ff.

51 Klemperer, *Tagebücher*, 437.

52 Ibid., 537.

53 Michael Rohde, *Von Muskau bis Konstantinopel: Eduard Petzold ein europäischer Gartenkünstler 1815-1891*, Muskauer Schriften, vol. 2 (Dresden: Verlag der Kunst Dresden, 1998), 29.

54 Preface to Sylvia Kabus, "Zwischen Rose und Lindenbaum. Die Stadt versagte im Dritten Reich ihren jüdischen Bürgern Erholung im Rosental," *Leipziger Blätter*, no. 42 (2003): 45.

55 Letter from E. Müller to Mayor Rudolf Haake, August 27, 1937, quoted in Kabus, "Zwischen Rose und Lindenbaum," 45-46. Kabus offers numerous further examples from Leipzig of defamations of the Jewish population.

56 Quoted in ibid., 46.

57 Gruner, *Judenverfolgung*, 7.

58 Bruss, *Bremer Juden*, 133.

59 See, e.g., Sächsische Schlösserverwaltung, ed., *Der Große Garten zu Dresden. Gartenkunst in vier Jahrhunderten* (Dresden: Michael Sandstein Verlag, 2001). The conference papers include contributions on the changes in the use of the grounds in the nineteenth century and the postwar situation. In the closing contribution, damage to the gardens is documented with photographs and otherwise. The exclusion order for the Jewish population during the Nazi period mentioned by Klemperer is, however, not referred to.

Working Green:
Artists in Relation to Schreber Gardens
Brigitte Franzen

The origins of the Schreber garden are, surprisingly, bound up in the military as well as pedagogy and orthopedics and are therefore significant for Germany from the middle to the end of the nineteenth century. Daniel Gottlieb Moritz Schreber, who was the namesake for Schreber gardens, was born in Leipzig in 1808. In his main work, *Kallipädie*, also known as *Education to Beauty*,[1] he proposed to raise children "firm and active," keeping them away from any "seductive" comfort and flabbiness. For Schreber, to stand up straight not only had a medical value but symbolized a morality, an attitude and mentality. To reach the goal of an upright person, he invented several instruments and exercises. There were "the Bridge," "the Head Holder," and "the Straight Holder" or "Shoulder Tie" (figs. 1–3). Schreber became especially popular for the Straight Holder, an instrument for sitting upright at a table while writing or reading. It was designed in the form of a horizontal figure eight that you had to slip into and which tied your shoulders back to keep them from "falling." A horizontal stick, mounted on the table in front of the child, pushed against the breastbone and caused discomfort when the head and the body fell forward. The Bridge was a veritable martial-arts exercise. The head and feet lay on chairs while the delinquent had to balance his body in the air. Such ideas derived from an interest in the natural sciences and a specific understanding of the human body as more or less formless. This formlessness had to be shaped, trained, and rectified for the sake of a straight-line personality.

Schreber exercised regularly with his five children. He was so extreme in this regime that by the time his younger son turned forty-two years old he had developed severe psychological problems. In his sixties, Daniel Paul Schreber wrote of his experiences in *Memoirs of My Nervous Illness*.[2] In the book he described problems with his father and his education and questioned under which conditions the mentally ill are to be committed against their will. The case of Daniel Paul Schreber became famous in psychoanalytic literature. Morton Schatzman, in particular, showed the interconnection between the son's paranoia and the father's mechanical apparatuses, referring to the house-tyranny of which Daniel had accused Moritz.[3] Even so, the elder Schreber was well aware of problems with his instruments, and he advised his colleagues to use the Straight Holder

only in grave cases, after gymnastics and other exercise had failed.

Moritz Schreber was an sportive man and helped found the Leipziger Turnverein, a club where prominent citizens of Leipzig came together for exercising in nature. Every morning at "six o'clock the men met to exercise in one of their friend's stepfather's gardens on Island Street."[4] To be a *Turner*—a gymnast—in Saxony in the 1830s, '40s, or '50s was still a political statement towards a more revolutionary national perspective. To be "National" at that time was a liberal position, because Germany as a national state did not yet exist; it was an agglomeration of several states, each with its own customs and legal and tax systems.

For a later generation of Schreber gardeners, Moritz Schreber was an intellectual-philosophical figure, somebody whose opinions and lifestyle they shared, a man who showed the ideals of a "character without falsehood," as a biographer in the 1920s put it, a "father of the Schreber Associations."[5] The first Schreber Association (*Schreberverein*) was founded by Ernst Hauschild in Leipzig in 1864, the same year Abraham Lincoln declared Yosemite the first national park of the United States. Schreber Associations in Saxony were pedagogic clubs that organized lectures, built libraries, and erected playgrounds. Hauschild published in his school newsletter of 1862 a text by Moritz Schreber on playgrounds that proposed the *Schreberplatz*, an area for play and sport in schools, and in 1865 the first Schreber Association acquired a meadow, which they called a *Schreberplatz*. Three years later, alongside the meadow, little gardens for children were established that the parents subsequently adopted. But it took quite a while before the gardens became really popular. In 1874 Leipzig established its second association. By 1891 there were six, and around the turn of the century these gardens boomed all over Germany. Eventually, they were called *Kleingärten*—little gardens—which included "workers' gardens," "Schreber gardens," "family gardens," and others.[6]

It is evident that the gardens were a reaction to or result of the Industrial Revolution. They provided the poor and the working class with recoverable land to work for their own sustenance. Today the German word *Schrebergarten* has become synonymous with all kinds of small gardens organized by clubs and

Queens Museum of Art
Down the Garden Path

Chapter 3
Essays

Figs. 1–3 Examples of Moritz
Schreber's *"Erziehungsapparate"*
(Machines for Education). (clock-
wise from top left) The Bridge,
the Straight Holder, and the Head
Holder. From Moritz Schreber,
Kallipädie (1858).

{133}

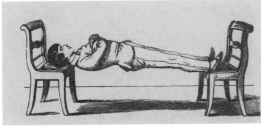

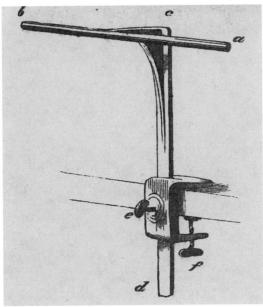

associations. For the broader public, Schreber's theories are no longer apparent. The connections between the "real" Moritz Schreber and the gardens named after him are more or less metaphoric. While his educational instruments relate to means of plant production and growth—tomatoes and beans are planted with sticks to climb up, a gerbera flower needs the help of a wire to stand upright—these analogies have a stronger meaning when one asks about the German disposition towards nature and "natural" education in the middle of the nineteenth century. On the other hand, the ideals of Schreber's educational principles were used in establishing rules for Schreber Associations. The aim to behave in an "upright," "sane," or "truthful" manner found accordance in Weimar Republic reformist circles and in the National Socialist ideology of the 1930s and '40s. The fact that Moritz Schreber's two sons had severe mental problems—Gustav, the eldest, committed suicide; the second, Paul, became psychotic—was overlooked.

The ambivalence of the Schreber biographies is also mirrored in the history of some of the Schreber Associations and their gardens. The relationship of the associations and their gardeners as general tenants of garden territories declined in the early twentieth century because of strict rules, which included, for example, the necessity for buying certain amounts of alcohol and other goods from the association, which did not suit sober personalities.[7] Nonetheless the gardens were successful. In 1915, in Berlin alone, there were 159 clubs with 13,000 members. In 1830 another, smaller urban-garden movement began when Kiel, a city on Germany's northern coast, created the first urban gardens, called "social gardens," and soon after, in 1833, the city of Berlin leased 143 workers' gardens to provide recreation ground for people with low income.[8] This development was due to influence from Great Britain.

Today gardens rooted in the Schreber tradition are places of popular aesthetics, representing a consumerist attitude and engagement. For perfectionists, living outdoors revolves around garden and hut equipment. Urban agriculture, on the other hand, is seriously discussed in the field of urban planning and in relation to the processes of shrinking cities.[9] Hopes are identified and gardens are planned, also in intercultural contexts, as demonstrated by the successful initiative Interkulturelle Gärten.[10] Nowadays patchwork economies in Germany and elsewhere require more and more intensive use of public land, as they did after the First World War, during the early Weimar Republic, and after the Second World War. This poses many questions concerning society, working conditions, land use, public aesthetics, neighborhood activism, and economic traditions. Urban agriculture has become a model for the postindustrial

development of cities worldwide, which must be read in the context of a critique of globalization.

The Schreber garden has held a place in vanguard modernity. Bertolt Brecht, together with Ernst Ottwald, conceived the 1932 movie *Kuhle Wampe oder Wem gehört die Welt?* (Kuhle Wampe, or Who Owns the World?), directed by Slatan Dudow with music by Hans Eisler. In the film, Dudow depicts the Schreber garden as a place for political activism and critique from the Left. The first version of the film was forbidden in the late Weimar Republic. In his *Ästhetik des Widerstandes* (The Aesthetics of Resistance, three vols., 1975, 1978, and 1981), Peter Weiss identifies the gardens, often called *Parzelle* in a northern German context, as stable islands and conspiratorial territories against Nazi troops and politics.

The Munich Garden of Cultures association provides a good example for the directions of newer and politically different "Schreber" ideas. Their aim is to provide grounding for immigrants, to give them a new perspective. One of the group's publications, a booklet for sponsors and supporters, presents the case of a Bosnian woman and her three children, refugees of the war in ex-Yugoslavia, living on fifteen square meters for a period of seven years. For her, the garden was much more than a site for growing vegetables. It was a shelter and had therapeutic value.

On the surface none of this would seem to have much connection to art, but there are artists who are very interested in these practices and processes; first, because of the analogy to artist-initiated projects in the public domain, and second, because artists have social and political interests and want to contribute their knowledge as "art-workers" to help enhance the aesthetic appearance of neighborhood gardens. Furthermore, they are very well trained to deal with authorities, and the label "artwork" gives access to a much broader community. It can be used to make things possible. Park Fiction is such an initiative based in Hamburg–St. Pauli. It is well known within and outside the art world, having exhibited its garden project at Documenta 11 in Kassel in 2002. The investigations of Ingo Vetter and Annette Weisser are to be mentioned too. Their interest in neighborhood gardens was motivated by the idea of gardens as informal sites of critique, like Martha Rosler's *If You Lived Here*, a project she did near Tompkins Square Park in New York City in the late 1980s.[11] After developing garden-related art projects in a German context, Weisser and Vetter investigated urban agriculture in Detroit, taking it as a model for "bottom-up processes" in a shrinking city.

Queens Museum of Art
Down the Garden Path

Chapter 3
Essays

Figs. 4–6 Peter Fischli and
David Weiss, *Garten* (Garden),
1997. Installation views,
Skulptur. Projekte in Münster,
1997. Courtesy Matthew Marks
Gallery, New York. Photos:
Roman Mensing / artdoc.de

{135}

In their video *I Am Farming Humanity*, they gave a voice to Lee Burns, formerly one of the leading city farmers in Detroit.[12]

* * *

For the international public-art exhibition Skulptur. Projekte in Münster (1997), the Swiss duo Peter Fischli and David Weiss developed an idea for a small garden (figs. 4–6). They searched Münster for the right place and found an old garden that they rented from an elderly lady. The garden was primarily a lawn surrounded by a whimsical hedge. Some time ago, another gardener had clipped the hedge into the forms of animals. Fischli and Weiss let the bushes grow until the animals were almost unrecognizable. They destroyed the lawn to create several beds in which they asked a gardener familiar with ecological farming to plant flowers and crops for a purposeful coexistence. A little hut was installed, and after erecting a small bridge over a canal that divided the garden from the surrounding landscape, it was free to visit. Entering such a private terrain was both strange and familiar. The atmosphere was as if the gardener had just disappeared for a short time. The tools were left there, and the viewer immediately participated in the process of working, enjoying, creating, but without being included. Was this really an art site? Were we at the right location for an artwork within a public-art exhibition? This garden was reclaimed by the artists and later by exhibition visitors as an art terrain and as a *locus amoenus*; it was an art lab, highly metaphoric for Fischli and Weiss. A garden that doesn't want to be an art site reflects on the working conditions and situations of art production itself. It plays with the naturalness of "making art." The actual art itself arose more from the use of photographic material that the artists have collected from gardens for almost twenty years—in Münster and elsewhere—and have showed in subsequent exhibitions. The documentation of the processes of growing, ripening, and blooming is contradicted by the artists' performative artworks, in the use of contemporary cross-fading techniques in their slide installations. The garden for Fischli and Weiss is more of a source and a beginning for the real work. They gave visitors in Münster a chance to take a look at a possible plein air studio with an ironic twist. Schreber-garden ideas about order and pureness in the garden were for Fischli and Weiss no more than a paraphrase of fruitful work with the soil. The artists were antipathfinders in the jungle of definitions about what contemporary art might be. Cleverly, they showed a work of art that didn't look like a work of art but which was widely used and overwhelmingly beautiful, even in the eyes of the sternest critic.

Stan Douglas, on the other hand, took a different view of the Schreber-garden phenomenon after staying in Berlin on a grant in the mid-'90s. His interests began in Potsdam, a Baroque city dense with Schreber gardens. As an artist particularly compelled by the concept of *das Unheimliche* (the uncanny), he remembered the stories of German author E. T. A. Hoffmann, who published his collection *Nachtstücke/ Nocturnae* (Night Pieces) in 1817. One of these stories, "Der Sandmann" (1815), describes a young man whose father had a relationship with a strange alchemist named Coppelius. The father and the stranger occasionally tried to make gold in the family's living room. One day the son, Nathanael, who was spying on the older men, became crazy with panic at the idea of being discovered. His mother had always warned him and his siblings that they had to go to bed before the sandman arrived, and so the boys invented the story of a cruel sandman who would throw sand in their eyes and steal them to give to his own brood as food. They identified Coppelius as the sandman.

Later, the father left the apartment and disappeared. It was said that he had trouble in a bar and was killed in a fight. Then the strange Coppelius never returned. Nathanael accused himself of being responsible for his father's death. When he grew up, he fell in love with a beautiful young woman. Her father, Coppola, was very interested in the young man as a fiancé for the girl, Olimpia. Blind with love over the woman's beauty, the young man discovers too late that he had fallen in love with an artificial puppet, a robot. In his 1919 essay "The Uncanny," Sigmund Freud used Hoffmann's story as an example of one's own making—because it is a return—of a remembrance; a shadow of an early, repressed experience.

In Douglas's film *Der Sandmann*, 1994 (figs. 7 and 8), the story is told in retrospect by Nathanael's sister to her brother and to a friend and vice versa: There are three narrators of the Hoffmann story, completely transformed, in three letters read aloud in front of the camera by a young black man. Douglas locates his interpretation of the narrative in a Schreber garden. He uses only the frame of the Hoffmann tale. Here the sandman seems to be a genius inventor-gardener, who wants to grow asparagus in winter with the help of special machinery. As the film shows the narrator, the narrative of the Schreber garden is also "shown." While the camera turns 360 degrees the story continually turns. In between, the viewer sees the whole garden erected as a film set in Potsdam's former UFA studios (now DOKFILM studios), which were not only the birthplace of Germany's film industry but also the most important location for the production of Nazi propaganda movies. The horror and cynicism that lie at the center of the story, retold in a modern version and revealed by the discovery that the whole scene is part of a film set, is troubling for the viewer. Several layers of interpretation are immediately evident, but instead of giving the viewer the security of insight, the film confuses. The garden is the scenario of horror. It contains the secret of privacy or freedom in a society of hypercontrol, like a Schreber Association. In Douglas's film, when the boys grew up to be men, they realized their mistake. Coppelius, whom they had accused of being the legendary sandman, was just a slightly mad inventor who used the garden as a laboratory. In so doing, he aroused the suspicion of outsiders, who believed that under the beautiful and orderly green surface of a Schreber garden—this so-called normality—lay distrust, horror, and cruelty. On the other hand, someone who tries to develop his idea of civilization in a broader sense, if only by raising asparagus in winter, finds no real place in a world of control.

The works described above are examples of what I call "fourth nature," a term I use to explain the position of gardens in contemporary art.[13] Within discourses on the relation of nature, gardens, and art, the ancient philosopher and politician Cicero claimed the term "second nature" for designed and rebuilt nature in the form of canalized rivers or agriculture. Jacopo Bonfadio, a late-Renaissance garden artist of the mid-sixteenth century, invented the description of a "third nature" for garden art, work which stands between art and nature and is part of both. The contemporary artist's relationship towards a first, second, or even third nature is complex, broken and mediated as it is by photography, film, video, and computerized images. The garden, artwork as well as art site, is highly open for metaphor and critique.

NOTES

1 Daniel Gottlieb Moritz Schreber, *Kallipädie oder Erziehung zur Schönheit durch naturgetreue und gleichmäßige Förderung normaler Körperbildung, lebenstüchtiger Gesundheit und geistiger Veredelung und insbesondere durch möglichst Benutzung spezieller Erziehungsmittel: Für Ältern, Erzieher und Lehrer* (Leipzig: Friedrich Fleischer, 1858).

2 Daniel Paul Schreber, *Denkwürdigkeiten eines Nervenkranken nebst Nachträgen und einem Anhang über die Frage: "Unter welchen Voraussetzungen darf eine für geisteskrank erachtete Person gegen ihren Willen in einer Heilanstalt festgehalten werden?"* (Leipzig: Oswald Mutze, 1903).

3 Morton Schatzman, *Soul Murder: Persecution in the Family* (London: Allen Lande and Harmondsworth, 1973); German edition, *Die Angst vor dem Vater. Langzeitwirkung einer Erziehungsmethode. Eine Analyse am Fall Schreber* (Reinbek bei Hamburg: Rowohlt, 1973). In his biography of the Schrebers, Han Israels doubts this opinion (see ch. 6, fn. 4) and states that the dialectics of the tyrant (in psychoanalysis) versus the paterfamilias (in Schreber-garden contexts) are typical for the perception of Moritz Schreber in the later literature. See Han Israels, *Schreber. Vater und Sohn. Eine Biographie* (Munich and Vienna: Verlag Internationale Psychoanalyse, 1989).

4 Richard G. Siegel, "Erinnerungen an Dr. Moritz Schreber: Nach Berichten von seinen Töchtern," in *Der Freund der Schreber Vereine*, no. 5 (1909), 205-09, see here 205. Quoted in Israels, *Schreber. Vater und Sohn*, 48.

5 Hugo Fritzsche, "Aus Dr. Moritz Schrebers Leben," in *Garten und Kind. Zeitschrift der mitteldeutschen Schrebergärtner*, no. 6 (1926), 12-14. Quoted in Israels, *Schreber. Vater und Sohn*, 65.

6 For more information, see Israels, *Schreber. Vater und Sohn*, 209.

7 See Rita Pohle-Schöttler, "Der Schrebergarten als Ort ästhetischen Handelns," Ph.D. dissertation, University of Stuttgart, 1993, 35.

8 George K. Lewis, "The Kleingärten: Evolution of an Urban Retreat," in *Landscape* 23, no. 2 (1979), 33.

9 See *Schrumpfende Städte, Band 1: Internationale Untersuchung*, exh. cat., ed. Philipp Oswalt (Berlin: Kunstwerke Institute for Contemporary Art; Ostfildern-Ruit: Hatje Cantz, 2004), or www.shrinkingcities.com.

10 See www.stiftung-interkultur.de.

11 Martha Rosler, *If You Lived Here: The City in Art, Theory and Social Activism*, ed. Brian Wallis (Seattle: Bay Press, 1991).

12 Ingo Vetter and Annette Weisser, *I Am Farming Humanity*, 2000, video, 16 min. See also Ingo Vetter, "Urbane Landwirtschaft. 'You have to build it to prove it!'" in *Schrumpfende Städte, Band 1*, 484-93.

13 Brigitte Franzen, *Die vierte Natur. Gärten in der zeitgenössischen Kunst* (Cologne: Walther Koenig, 2000).

Queens Museum of Art
Down the Garden Path

Chapter 3
Essays

Figs. 7 and 8 On the set of Stan
Douglas's *Der Sandmann*,
DOKFILM studios, Potsdam,
December 1994.

{137}

Chapter 4
Interviews and
Project Essays

A Conversation with Alan Sonfist
Valerie Smith

Time Landscape is an artwork by Alan Sonfist located on the corner of LaGuardia Place and Houston Street in Manhattan. It was conceived as the first in a series of precolonial landscapes that would reintroduce the natural history of the site to the community, citizens and visitors alike. The original topography of the quarter-acre rectangle and the heirloom varieties of natural species planted there were researched by Sonfist in the city's historical records. *Time Landscape* was completed under the administration of Mayor Ed Koch, in 1978; Sonfist proposed it to the city, however, in 1965, which makes it the first urban Earthwork of its generation.

Valerie Smith How did *Time Landscape* come about?

Alan Sonfist It was a long and winding trail. Doris Freedman, who founded the Public Arts Council and later became New York City's director of Cultural Affairs, gave me spiritual support early on but didn't know how to implement the project. The Parks Department said the same thing: "It's a great idea. We don't know anything beyond that."

Naively, I went to the museums. Tom Hoving, the director of the Metropolitan Museum of Art, and Arthur Rosenblatt, the Met's architect for many years, became strong supporters. Out of that contact they invited me to do a landscape project for the museum expansion in Central Park. As *Time Landscape* started gaining credibility, Hoving introduced me to other potential sponsors. David Rockefeller personally supported the project, and Bob Rosenblum, who wrote the introduction to my recent book (*Alan Sonfist: Nature—The End of Art* [Gli Ori, 2004]), was an advocate of my work. Around that time I got invited to do research at MIT because they had heard of *Time Landscape*. That opportunity gave me fresh insight into the relationship between art and science, which has always been key to my work. And I received great support from private individuals such as Sandra Gilman and Linda Macklowe who were ahead of their time in understanding the importance of environmental art. These are all people I respect; they understand history. So everyone was excited about the idea of doing a historical landscape in the city. But there was no structure in place to support it.

I was living on Thirteenth Street and quickly became aware of community boards. The Greenwich Village Community Board wanted to realize the project, so I made a presentation to them. They voted it in and selected the site in 1969. Then I met with the commissioners at least once or twice a month. The meetings scared them because they couldn't understand the concept of creating a forest in the city, but I had leading environmentalists and historians consulting on the project—the Village board would never have made a commitment to it if I hadn't developed a strong group around the work. If someone said to me today, "Alan, you were very calculating. You didn't give up. You started to build this momentum of support so they couldn't deny you," I would realize intuitively that this was what I was doing, but logically I was not aware of it. In addition to the congressmen, senators, and Parks Department, I had strong support for the project; I just didn't have the know-how to change the minds of commissioners who were appointed into these positions. After a series of communications, I started to realize I was on my own to actually create a new vocabulary for public art.

Eventually the commissioners approved it. The comfort zone for them was the idea of a park with trees. But I'll never forget what one said to me—"This has never been done, why do you want to do it?" Obviously my response was "That's why I want to do it!" I was too naive, too young, which was lucky. The commissioners were being very diplomatic. They absolutely did not want it to happen, but they would never say no. I could understand their dilemma. I was this kid with a wild idea. They must have thought, "We're not going to give this guy a piece of city land under our signature!"

VS Why is the beginning date for *Time Landscape* given as 1965? How long was the process all together?

AS The initial proposal and drawings were delivered to the Parks Department in 1965. They eventually all changed. It took over ten years for me to navigate it into a physical reality.

The turning point was the election of Ed Koch. The commissioners didn't care about the project, they were constantly delaying it. But when Koch became mayor in 1978, they knew that he would push the project through, and my fantasy is that that is why they all approved it.

Queens Museum of Art
Down the Garden Path

Chapter 4
Interviews and
Project Essays

(clockwise from top left)
Alan Sonfist
Hidden Lake Landscape, 1965
Graphite on paper, 10 x 12 inches
Private collection

Alan Sonfist
Hidden Farm Landscape, 1965

Graphite on paper, 10 x 12 inches
Private collection

Alan Sonfist
*Hidden Rock-Geologic
Landscape*, 1965
Graphite on paper, 10 x 12 inches
Private collection

Alan Sonfist
Hidden Seashores Landscape,
1965
Graphite on paper, 10 x 12 inches
Private collection

Alan Sonfist
Hidden Fruit Landscape, 1965

Graphite on paper, 10 x 12 inches
Private collection

Alan Sonfist
Hidden Mix Forest Landscape,
1965
Graphite on paper, 10 x 12 inches
Private collection

{141}

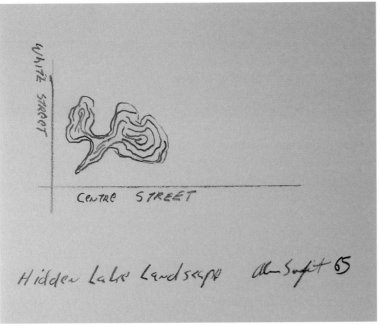

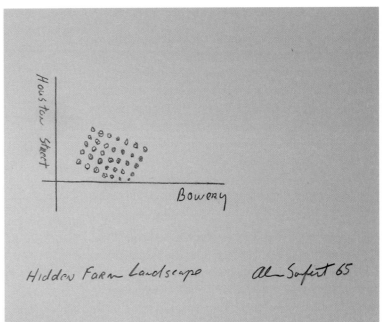

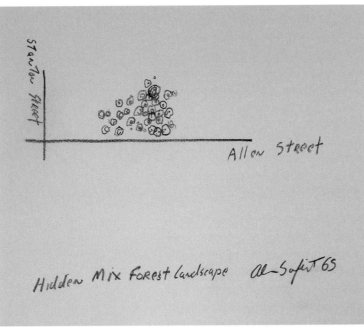

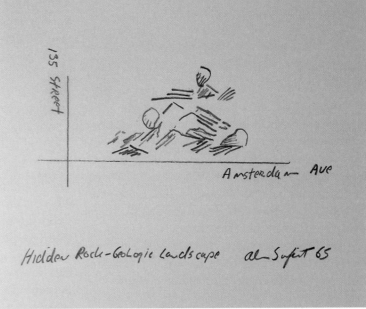

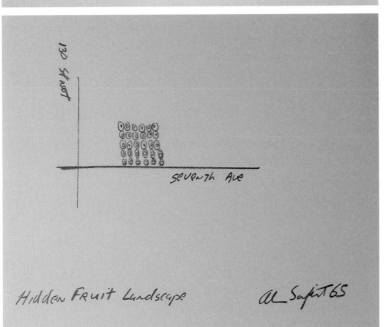

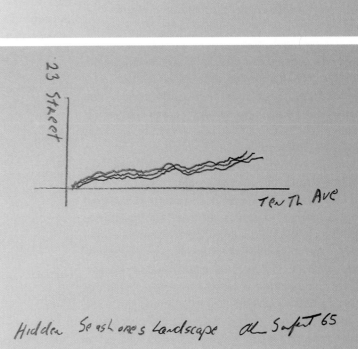

VS How did you get to know him and gain his support?

AS I started meeting wonderful people who were strong advocates of the environment. Ed Koch, who was concerned about the Village, supported them, and he himself felt it was going to be an important contribution to the community. He is not the type of person who would ever endorse anything he didn't like. The Village planning board saw my determination.

VS Even today it takes a long time to get the authorities to give their stamp of approval for artists who want to do major interventions in the city.

AS The ironic part of it is that right after *Time Landscape* finished, the door opened. The commissioners of the highway system were in all the newspapers because they had created this project. It made almost every major television network. They were so happy. And they started endorsing anything that came to their doorsteps labeled as art. But that quickly shut down.

VS Tell me the specifics about the concept of *Time Landscape*. You had wanted to do more than just one location.

AS I had originally proposed fifty sites throughout the city, all with different time frames. The idea was to introduce a visitor to the city and to show how each site would have looked during the transition between the indigenous people and the Europeans. The Village in particular had a long history of interconnection between the two populations. These projects are still on the city's books.

I gleaned what turned out to be idealized information from early Dutch and English logging records of that area and early maps of the city. There were accounts about how they removed groves of oak for timber. They mentioned a stream along Minetta Lane only a few blocks away from the site at LaGuardia and Houston. The English description of this region indicated a famous trout stream off Broadway. They wrote about taking naps in a beech grove. Early topographical maps show that area was hilly, so I constructed a beech grove on a hill.

I did a series of drawings dealing with the lost streams, wetlands, meadows, ponds, lakes, forests, and other natural features of the city that had long since disappeared, and a series of topographical mappings. Then I laid out patterns with indigenous seeds. The streams would have shown the beginnings of the island's evolution from a geological point of view. This would have meant exposing marshlands, which obviously was not met with enthusiasm on the Lower East Side or other areas in the city where there were marshlands. There are also springs. In the bottom of my building there's a well which has been

sealed, because in the 1900s, when yellow fever broke out, the city forbade people to drink New York City water. The whole structure still exists, either in the sewage systems of the city or in some of the subway systems where there are often floods. Canal Street was a stream before it was a canal. You can see the buildings sagging right into Canal Street.

Early on, I did drawings on paper that show the whole network of rivers and how the city diverted water to create a reservoir. They include photographs tracing the rivers of New York City for the first Earth Day in 1970. I was trying to expose the rivers, but it was more of a symbolic gesture because they have all disappeared under the concrete. By that time Parks had become an advocate of my work and endorsed the concept of the forest.

VS You think of *Time Landscape* as a forest? I think of it as a garden because it's enclosed.

AS You have to think of a city as being this very precious environment where you create these small vistas of forests and buildings as part of the forest. The buildings are the tall trees like in a mature forest. How they affect other specimens that are interacting with them is part of the environment that you're creating. Everything is metaphoric.

VS What native seeds and plants were available in that time period? You hear about heritage horticulture now, but in the 1960s it didn't exist.

AS I studied different specimens. In addition to wildflowers, there were trees. The highest planted was three feet; the smallest ones were little six-inch seedlings, and amazingly they're now thirty, fifty feet tall. It was a daunting experience trying to find the correct ones. I convinced a couple of nurseries in New Jersey, who were at that time growing native specimens, to begin to sell them. When I began the project, no one grew heritage plants commercially. Now they are profitable, and they're getting commissions from other artists and landscape architects, so I'm very pleased. It's still what I would consider to be the edge of landscaping and especially the edge of art. Research laboratories and universities are constantly adjusting their ideas about how these specimens survive in a city. It is important that *Time Landscape* has become a functioning part of the community, not just a decoration that's been stuck there.

VS Why was it important for you to pursue this project?

AS As a child I witnessed a primal forest being destroyed. I grew up in the South Central Bronx, and in that section of the Bronx River there were fox

Queens Museum of Art
Down the Garden Path

Chapter 4
Interviews and
Project Essays

{143}

and deer and small farms. Unimaginable as it seems, it was not a hundred years ago but only forty or even thirty years ago that this landscape still existed in the Bronx. But it rapidly disappeared. By the time the 1960s hit, the Bronx was burning and everything was being destroyed, including my forest. They decided it was dangerous and poured concrete over it.

A nice thing happened under Henry Stern, the former parks commissioner under Koch and Giuliani. He landmarked *Time Landscape*, making it an icon for the city. I'm very pleased about this because I wasn't aware that contemporary art could have such a demarcation. Stern also introduced the concept of historical restoration to parks throughout the city, which included the section of the Bronx River that I played in as a child.

VS What was your relationship with other artists of your generation? Did you know, for instance, Gordon Matta-Clark or Robert Smithson? Who were the artists you hung out with?

AS In 1968 or 1969 I was involved with a wonderful individual, Ted Kheel. He was an environmental and labor advocate. He invited a group of artists to meet and promote the development of mass transit. This is when they were trying to overcome the highway lobbyist groups, and he wanted to get people involved in the social issues of the time. He invited me and Smithson—and during the first meetings Rauschenberg, whom I admired, was part of it—so we all got to know each other.

The idea of the meetings was to discuss our work and various proposals and create a series of print editions to help support the mass-transit lobbyist group. By then I was already in the planning stages of *Time Landscape*. Smithson was much older than me. I was in my early twenties, and he was in his thirties. It's interesting—he wouldn't talk to me. He found me to be a real threat. He knew what I was doing, but he didn't want to acknowledge it.

I felt the other artists were all more conservative. I was interested in the concept of trying to do something for society. I have a different approach. I've always been committed to the environment. Whether or not it's art has never been relevant to me; it's more how the symbol functions in our society. Labels come afterwards.

VS But did you have any artist friends who were like-minded? Or did you feel really out on a limb, so to speak?

AS I didn't have any artist friends [*laughs*]. I was involved with environmentalists, city planners, art historians, people who thought beyond the crafted object. One of my best friends—we knew each other

as students—is a cancer researcher who has just developed a vaccine for skin cancer. Within the next five years it will be on the market. He's devoted his whole life to this. The people I engage with are those people whose work is beneficial to the environment, which includes us.

But I'm also part of the art world. I knew Gordon Matta-Clark later on. I was involved with him at 112 Greene Street [the SoHo artists' space of which Matta-Clark was a board member], where I did a show, and he was one of the sponsors. He was a wonderful person whose work I admired. I definitely felt he contributed a wonderful thought-process in the art world—again, a totally different approach. There's room for many different interpretations. I don't believe that one person has the only answer to the world. It's scary when people think that. But the big difference between me and people like Smithson is that I was committed to urban centers. I always made it very clear from day one that I would not interfere with or try to improve primal landscape areas. But I *would* create an artwork in an environment where land had been altered by humans. There a dynamic is set up between the primal landscape and what it has become through social intervention.

VS Smithson conceptualized a project called *Floating Island to Travel Around Manhattan Island* in 1970. He also wrote an article about Frederick Law Olmsted's Central Park. My theory is that the project had to do with a bit of park landscape or forested area recreated on a barge that was to tour around Manhattan. It seems that there may be a connection between *Time Landscape* and Smithson's unrealized barge project.

AS I don't know. The first proposals I did were in the mid-1960s. It would be interesting to see how that related, because he wouldn't talk to me when I first proposed my forest project.

VS But what about the acknowledgment and support of the art world?

AS [*Laughs.*] I think it takes a long time for the art world to catch up to what is art. The art world in the 1960s was very small. Art world, non-art world, it doesn't matter to me. I was definitely not embraced by the commercial art world. Tom Hoving, and Tom Messer at the Guggenheim Museum, embraced the work. They were part of the more enlightened or educated art world. The reality is that you have to have a vision, and people often find this hard to understand initially. I don't think back. During the 1970s it was a disaster, like all efforts to introduce new vision into art. Would I have liked it to be endorsed by other artists? Of course I would have. It would have been more fun.

(top row, left to right)
Alan Sonfist
Ecological Playground (detail),
2005
Graphite on paper, 22 x 30 inches
Private collection

Alan Sonfist
Nature Theater, 1999
Graphite on paper, 22 x 30 inches
Study for installation at
Künstlergarten Weimar, Germany
Private collection

Alan Sonfist
Healing Trail (detail), 2005
Graphite on paper, 22 x 30 inches
Study for garden at Royal Victoria
Hospital, Barrie, Canada
Private collection

(center rows)
Alan Sonfist
Healing Trails (details), 2005
Graphite on paper,
22 x 30 inches each
Studies for garden at Royal
Victoria Hospital, Barrie, Canada
Private collection

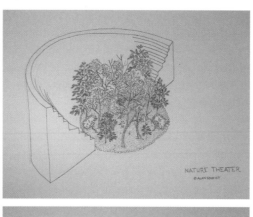

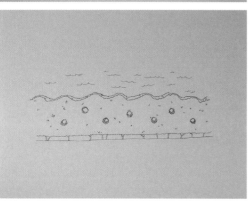

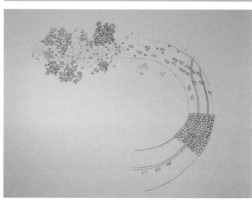

VS When did you work with Leo Castelli?

AS My relationship with the gallery had a strange, schizophrenic feeling. I met him in the late 1960s, and he really wanted to show my work. But I was extremely shy and didn't talk to him again for several years. Eventually I did a show with him in the early 1970s. He was a visionary. There are people in the art world that can take something and make it happen, but they are very few and far between.

VS What kind of work were you doing at that point?

AS At Castelli, I showed photo-landscapes. Making objects and taking photographs have always been an intrinsic part of my life. I developed the skill to draw realistically or abstractly, so I didn't need to go to art school to learn the craft. Actually, my objective at the university was to get away from it. I went to an agricultural school originally. The farthest thing from my mind was to study art, because I'd been doing it since I was a child, I just never labeled it as such. It is a fun thing to do, which puts me in a strange position when painting is referred to as a struggle. Working with human beings is a struggle. Doing a massive public project and making it succeed—in the sense of communicating with people—is a struggle.

   In the 1970s, when I showed at 112 Greene Street, the work was very well respected. It was great. A group of people on the board selected me to do a show. My mother had saved every single photograph and drawing I ever did, which is wonderful, so I showed the drawings with maps that traced the history of New York City as it was observed by the earliest explorers. I paralleled early engravings with my drawings, and showed a progression up to my most recent images. These maps were a mixture of science and fantasy. I was trying to show how we understand an evolving urban environment and our own landscape.

VS How was the exhibition received?

AS It was kind of funny. I didn't care. It always fascinated me why some art magazines would say, "These are the hot artists, these are the great artists of this time period." If you go back and look at these artists, they don't exist. I don't justify what I did because I wanted the art world to give me applause. They were probably terrified of what I was doing. Almost every show I had during that time was written up in the *New York Times*. There were a few critics who could understand the philosophical reason behind the work and got involved in these concepts that weren't being taught in academia. Now it's part of the curriculum. Probably now that *Nature—The End of Art* is out, because these ideas are being rediscussed, you will see them reappear in other formats. From my perspective, the environment is the only major art movement from the last part of the century.

VS But if you were so shy, Alan, how could they be terrified?

AS Oh, I had a long beard and long hair. I didn't verbalize as much as I'm doing now. I did make very strong statements early on. I feel very fortunate to have known the people I did then and that they backed me. If you don't know the structure, you are able to operate more freely, but when you start to understand the system, or at least think you understand it, you create more restrictions for yourself. I still believe, to a certain extent, that everything is possible. For instance, who would think a kid from the Bronx would be doing a project for Prince Richard of Westphalia, advising him on how to redevelop his property? It's magical to me. It's a dream to think that I am dealing with the living royalty of Europe, reintroducing them to their ancestral heritage. It's an adventure. I'm pushing the edges of landscaping further back because it's now become almost a vocabulary among landscapers and artists.

VS Tell me about the project for the German prince.

AS The project is in Westphalia, outside of Cologne. I created a Neolithic landscape. I'm selecting plants for both historical as well as visual reasons. We came up with over a hundred specimens to reintroduce that had migrated outside of Germany, as far as China. I started to do this kind of project in Tampa in the early 1990s. I created an ice-age landscape there for them. To me this is what art is. It's pushing the edge of what we can comprehend visually and mentally.

VS Is there anything left growing naturally from that time?

AS There are ferns and lower specimens. I'm currently concerned with trees that are under stress in our environment today such as oaks and maples. The earth is experiencing a strong transition. It's shocking that we want the oak tree to be a major American symbol when the conditions in our environment are becoming hostile to it. My work is about trying to understand that in these transitions, there are alternatives. I'm selecting alternative species that historically existed on the site and which are again becoming compatible to the contemporary environmental conditions. This turns the idea of time upside down and uses it as part of the evolutionary process. It is a shift of aesthetic understanding. I'm in a whole new realm of thought.

This interview took place December 22, 2004, in New York.

A Conversation with Brian Tolle and Diana Balmori
Valerie Smith

With *Skid Rows*, artist Brian Tolle and landscaper Diana Balmori won a competition to create a temporary garden as part of the exhibition "Down the Garden Path." Balmori, best known for the World Financial Center Winter Garden in New York and NTT Shinjuku Headquarters Plaza in Tokyo, and Tolle, the creator of the Irish Hunger Memorial in New York, have in previous collaborations proposed a green solution to pedestrian and vehicular traffic for the Queens Plaza subway station and waterfront reclamation for a polluted area of Chicago's public beaches. In both cases the goal was public space aesthetically and sustainably resolved.

So too with *Skid Rows*, a playful but environmentally healthy new method of horticulture: A hot-dogging pickup truck acts as a low-impact cultivator, seeding an open, grassy area of the Queens Botanical Garden with an array of poppies and tickseeds. The use of the truck both allows the creation of patterns large enough to be seen from planes landing at LaGuardia Airport and updates the tradition of *parterres de broderie*—all while inverting the truck's ecologically negative connotations.

Valerie Smith How do you two collaborate across the boundaries of landscape architecture and sculpture? What's your working method?

Diana Balmori Collaboration has been easy and enjoyable for both of us. Brian's ability to concentrate on a problem is perhaps what makes working with him most valuable. It is a trait I share and one that allows the work to develop quickly. I'd say that Brian and I have reached results both in Chicago and in our two projects in Queens that actually splice our professions together.

Brian Tolle When Diana and I made a proposal for the redevelopment of Queens Plaza, the most important issue for her was sustainability in a harsh environment. If I had arrived there alone, the question of which plants might survive in such a place and how we might make use of water from runoff would not necessarily have been part of the equation—I saw the water as a sculptural element where a certain form or gesture might happen or a certain light might occur. But when we combined our thoughts, we ended up with a new way of thinking about the site and created a hybrid discipline.

People often make the mistake of asserting themselves as professionals in other fields in which they have little or no training. Artists move easily between disciplines as part of their practices, whether they're designing furniture or cooking food in a gallery. If you're deluded into thinking that you actually are a chef, then you've lost the art. And you probably end up being a pretty mediocre chef on top of that.

DB Everything we are saying with assurance now about *Skid Rows* was tentative at the beginning of the project. There was a long exchange of ideas and many discussions. For instance, sustainability was not our primary aim, but it served as a means to establish a working method through which to get to a form. It was a way of going at the idea of making a garden.

VS Can you talk about *Skid Rows* a little bit more, and describe its impetus?

BT *Skid Rows* was born out of personal experience. My partner and I have a house in the Catskills. We are often confronted by people who drive all-terrain vehicles (ATVs), which not only create noise pollution but tear up the landscape as well. I find myself being pretty judgmental on the one hand and envious on the other: I go upstate for serenity and some jackass comes plowing through the woods on a snowmobile. At the same time, it looks like they're having a heck of a lot of fun.

One of Diana's priorities is getting rid of the vast expanses of fertilized, mown lawn that are rolling over the suburbs—just think about places like Flushing Meadows! She also wants to develop more diverse plantings in urban environments. So she's concerned with these issues; meanwhile I've got this experience with ATVs and trucks. Together we started discussing how to use our different experiences and training to put forward productive ways of thinking about the environment.

VS When you described those guys with their trucks, I had an image of Michael Heizer and others playing these macho roles, dashing out in their trucks to move the earth. How is *Skid Rows* different from that kind of Earthworks project?

DB This project is about the garden, which is a cultural approach to the land that has a long and rich history. For example, the Victorian culture of "bedding out" plants to create a garden was a response

Queens Museum of Art
Down the Garden Path

Chapter 4
Interviews and
Project Essays

Brian Tolle and Diana Balmori
Skid Rows, 2005
Performance views,
Queens Botanical Garden,
New York, May 2005
Courtesy of the artists

{147}

to industrialization, and to the industrial-scale production of plants that were planted for their short blooming period, then thrown out and replaced by another blooming plant. Using a truck in order to create a garden seems antithetical and might be seen wrongly as a continuation of the Earthworks movement. But the way we use the truck is different. We are not using it to move earth. Nor are we using it to plow, because plowing breaks the structure of the soil and you lose nutrients and soil to the air. Instead, the truck will be used as a seeder using the new method of direct sowing. So *Skid Rows* is bringing about a change in the way a garden is produced.

BT Not to be too critical of anyone, but we city slickers often judge people who have a good old time going out in a field with their pickup trucks, revving their engines, spinning their wheels and doing doughnuts. A slight attitude adjustment might enable us to think instead, "Gee, I'm sure they're having a great time, it's recreation, but there is unfortunately a negative impact on the environment." So what happens if we turn off-roading on its head? We channel that energy to serve the environment and create an enormous line drawing. Once we understood that the work was a kind of drawing, we went back and researched traditional French *broderie.*

DB *Parterres de broderie* are very intricate geometrical layouts whose patterns are taken from embroidery; hence the name. You can do this with a truck.

BT There's an element of the spectacle, too, like in NASCAR or truck pulls at the county fair. *Skid Rows* has entertainment value, but in the service of the most advanced planting techniques and a new mode of expression. In the end, you don't get a big car crash or explosion. It won't be very exciting. Once the event is over, you're left with these lines in the ground, and if you were to happen to come back in a month or two, something will have happened. Instead of ruts, there will be a garden.

VS Right now you're both emphasizing the linear, drawinglike aspects of *Skid Rows*. But what about sculptural ways of landscaping? Diana, how does your philosophy of landscape architecture relate to more sculptural approaches?

DB There can be a sculptural intention in creating forms in landscaping; yet the main intention is not one of creating sculpture. That aim should come only after making the landscape fit for human use and enjoyment. The same is true of architecture. A building can be sculptural, but it has to work as a building.

BT The worst-case scenario is when a landscape architect understands the earthwork or the art

object purely in aesthetic terms—seeing the trench or pit purely for the way the form looks in the landscape as opposed to understanding why an artist might dig into the landscape in the first place. It's the appearance without the concept. On the flipside, the same disconnect is true for artists who make a move that comes out of a specific tradition within landscape architecture which is done purely for the way it appears. There the artist makes a false assumption about function.

VS I'm going to throw out a couple of names: Herbert Bayer and Charles Jencks.

DB Oh, those are beautiful examples. Herbert Bayer really got the point of the differences we're talking about. He moved from Bauhaus graphics to landforms as sculptures. Then in his Mill Creek Canyon Earthwork in Washington State [1979–82] he made a great leap. The hilly park had a stream coming down as an eroding torrent as a result of the surrounding area getting built up and paved. He sculpted the land to capture the water, slow it down, and store it when needed, and all his beautiful landforms were shaped for this purpose. His forms work and have a reason for being. *And* they are sculptural.

On the other hand, Charles Jencks's impetus and aim are mainly formal. His landforms are beautiful; he makes sculptures with the materials of landscape. In addition, he is working within a tradition in Renaissance gardens of sharply contoured, grassy landforms—Claremont, in England, is a good example of this kind of work. But those earthforms were used as amphitheaters. Jencks, who has a very good eye, is trying to dust off this tradition and renew it.

VS Do you see an increase in collaborations between landscape architects and artists? Michael Van Valkenburgh has worked with Ann Hamilton in New York's Battery Park and with Mel Bochner at Carnegie Mellon University in Pittsburgh; Paula Hayes worked with Rafael Viñoly at the Cleveland Museum of Art.

DB Yes, there is an increase in collaborations between landscape architects and artists. The collaborations are more visible and less rigidly separated than those between architects and landscape architects.

BT Artists and landscape architects in collaborative roles with architects are in a similar position. A lot of public-art projects are hitched to architecture; likewise, landscape opportunities, especially in urban centers, are often defined by architecture and are marginalized. We're not talking about working in vast sculpture parks like Sonsbeek in the Netherlands, or international exhibitions that are

Queens Museum of Art
Down the Garden Path

Chapter 4
Interviews and
Project Essays

{149}

geared towards experimentation. We have to negotiate and navigate around an architectural design and reckon with the architects.

VS How much of that has to do with economics?

DB It has an economic side, but it's more complex. Time is critical: The concept of the building precedes whatever the artist and the landscaper do, particularly when they're not part of siting. Siting makes an enormous difference in what you can do in landscape and in the relationship between landscape and architecture.

BT I'm working with the architect Hugh Hardy on a federal courthouse in Jackson, Mississippi, of which one-half percent of the budget has been allocated for art. I'm fortunate in that Hugh is an exception: He's open to the idea of me manipulating and influencing his design as opposed to saying, "Here's the building, you can work here but not there." Or "Bring in a sculpture; we'll put it there for you."

I'm a bit spoiled because of my experience with the Irish Hunger Memorial [2002]. I was invited to design an entire half-acre site in Lower Manhattan and was given the opportunity to choose the architect and landscape architect. It was an exceptional commission, where a project of that scope—five million dollars—was awarded to an artist. It was a radical shift in that the client, Timothy Carey of the Battery Park City Authority, wanted to develop a memorial project first and foremost as a major work of public art.

VS Roberto Burle Marx wondered why more landscape architects didn't think of themselves as artists. Isamu Noguchi hated the separation of the different art fields. Diana, do you think of yourself as unusual in that respect as compared to your colleagues?

DB I suppose I do. I identify with Noguchi's and Burle Marx's impatience with the divisions. Landscape is an art, but art and landscape are not the same. I draw, but my aim is not that of a painter—though I am as serious as any painter about what I put down on paper. I'm using the tools of another art to work in mine, but there is a fluidity in passing from one to another.

There are periods in history in which you find certain pieces, like Vaux-le-Vicomte in France, in which there really is an incredible play between the landscape, the architecture, and the sculpture. Back then landscapers had a very different relationship to art and architecture. With *Skid Rows* we're trying to find a different interpretation of what a garden can be and how its pieces work together.

VS The best view of *Skid Rows* would be from above. Did you design it for the airplanes going to LaGuardia?

BT We like the idea that the airport is right there.

VS But people who come to the botanical garden won't be able to see its two-dimensional, gestural aspect.

DB They will experience its spatial aspect, which is more important than the overall visual pattern from above.

BT The layering of the curves from ground level will be quite beautiful.

VS You are also introducing an element of chance in the composition of the garden by using the truck for the seeding.

BT That's right. A great deal of planning and experimentation went into designing this garden. That said, we can't really know what it will look like. Maybe you'll drive the truck or Diana will, and maybe your "drawing" style—your driving style—is different from her style which is different than mine. I got an automatic just in case, so different people can drive it. We might even drive it back to the Queens Museum and leave it there, depositing poppy seeds along the way.

This interview took place February 9, 2005, in New York.

The Kraus Campo:
Some Thoughts Behind the Garden
Mel Bochner

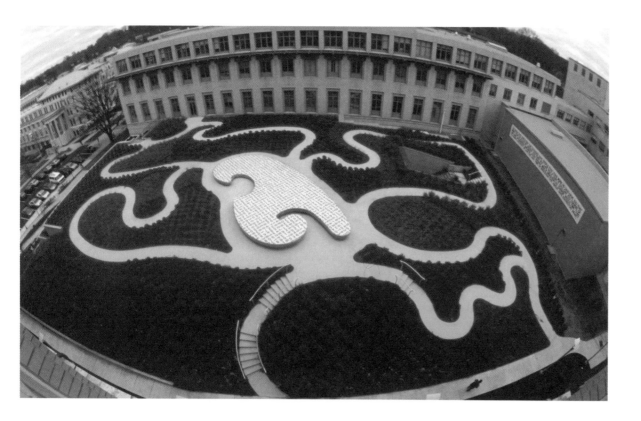

Over the past three years (2002-2004), I spent a great deal of time on the Carnegie Mellon University campus studying how students use the public/common spaces. What became apparent to me was that it was unnecessary to duplicate any existing outdoor areas. After talking to many people on campus I began to visualize a unique kind of garden. The original inspiration came from the Greek agora, an open marketplace where teachers of different philosophies held classes side by side, and where students could listen to their teachers debate, all while walking along. I imagined a place where walking and getting lost in conversation could become an active rather than a passive pleasure; a place to meet friends and colleagues, or encounter strangers from other disciplines . . . a literal marketplace of ideas.

As the project developed, I realized the site needed a center, a heart to circulate around (and a place to sit down and have lunch). The word *campo* comes from the Latin *campus*—an open field. The most famous campo is in the Italian city of Siena, which, with its streets radiating out from the center like the arms of a starfish, suggested a model for the garden. If Italian architecture seems foreign to Pittsburgh, remem-ber that the two greatest buildings in Pittsburgh are H. H. Richardson's Allegheny County Courthouse, an homage to medieval European architecture, and Henry Hornbostel's masterpiece the College of Fine Arts, which references an encyclopedic range of the great monuments of the world, among them the cathedrals of central Italy.

I collaborated on the design of the garden with Michael Van Valkenburgh. Both of us felt that the campus needed a space of fantasy and imagination, where one could escape from the daily pressures of academic life, somewhere not on the way to some-where else. That is what we tried to build—a place set apart, a world in itself. It has been suggested that the garden is "out of context" with the run of campus architecture, and that the colors "clash" with the neutral tones of adjacent buildings. But that design philosophy, with its subtext of "never call attention to yourself," has only littered the contemporary landscape with bland, unimaginative buildings.

In order to give the garden the feeling of being a world, it needed a central generating form. From the beginning I was certain that it had to be an organic form. How better to generate a set of curves than from the French curve? And what a happy coinci-

Queens Museum of Art
Down the Garden Path

Chapter 4
Interviews and
Project Essays

Mel Bochner and
Michael Van Valkenburgh
Kraus Campo, 2004
Carnegie Mellon University,
Pittsburgh
Courtesy of the artist
Photo: Heather Mull

{151}

dence that it resembled another historical signifier—
the artist's palette. That engineers and artists may
no longer use these tools does not alter their ability to symbolize two entire cultures at a glance.
Covering the French curve with numbers arranged in
a random pattern (with the additional twist of a four-
directional axial rotation) was inspired by the great
black-and-white Roman mosaic floors at Pompeii and
Herculaneum.

Our concept behind the paths was to choreograph
the experience of a long walk in a small space. The
meandering paths, rising and falling as they curve
between the undulating mounds, heighten one's
awareness of her constantly changing orientation to
the site, all while giving the surreal sensation of step-
ping into orange. The planting material was selected
to have color that changes in spectacular and surprising patterns as the seasons progress.

Inscribed in tile on the back wall is a quotation
from the philosopher Ludwig Wittgenstein. It has
been transcribed word for word in reverse order,
an old and simple form of encryption. The idea was
to provide a captionlike text to accompany the garden, but one that critiques the very idea of those
"elevated sentiments" engraved on institutional
facades around the world. The quotation, when deci-
phered, reveals itself as a metaphor for the garden
as a labyrinth.

I hope our design offers all the desirable pleasures
of a garden, including intellectual stimulation. But
even beyond that I hope that it offers students an
ideal to strive for—think for yourself, use your imagination, don't worry about blending in, and keep in
mind that sometimes you have to walk around in circles, or look at the world backwards, to see it as it
really is.

Paradise in the New World
Sergio Vega

Out of Tuscany

I woke up at noon, still tired and not too excited about getting out into the infernal heat. The activity on the street moved at high speed under the merciless sun. The city had a rough texture: unpainted walls, garbage on the sidewalks, loud street vendors. Enormous trees and exotic flowers contrasted with the toxic environment created by clouds of white automobile exhaust. After walking for almost an hour I found a restaurant; its walls featured painted murals of animals in a swamp. There was something of a prehistoric quality about these murals, which represented with an illustrational, postphotographic realism the epic battle for survival in the animal kingdom. Everyone in the restaurant, including the cook and the waiters, was absorbed in watching television. Carnival had ended the day before, and the votes of the hundreds of judges in charge of awarding the best *escolas de samba*[1] were counted on live television, nationwide. While I ate sprouts of palm salad, the silence broke and everybody started arguing; the winner turned out to be Mangueira,[2] followed very closely by Beija Flor.[3]

After coffee I boarded a city bus, which, roaring with deafening agony, took me around the dusty suburbs of the city. I disembarked at a favela that extended throughout a valley of ocher and orange, colors out of a postcard of the Tuscan countryside. The neighborhood surrounded a line of middle-class apartment buildings on top of the hill, parallel to a large avenue on the other side. Far from being pastoral, this panorama reflected a social logic, embodied in the topography of the landscape in a literally vertical manner: The houses of the rich stood on top, the houses of the poor lined the bottom.

The anti-aesthetic strategy of the shanty is the perversion of collage, a pragmatic logic in which the immediacy of function drastically subjugates form. The houses that are not made out of bricks are made out of cardboard boxes, advertisements, road signs, leftover industrial crates, car tires, tree branches, and plastic linings. The organic happening of the dwellings takes place in fragments, and although they are made out of previously disposed-of materials, nothing is really disposable since everything is transitory.[4]

Alice's Backyard

I walked into the shantytown; a bunch of skinny dogs that barely barked followed me. I found a decrepit garden with flowers growing between garbage and building materials. There were also rabbits and chickens among abandoned furniture and blankets drying in the sun. The site sustained a nightmarish chaos that lead me to envision the playground of an Alice that never made it back, abandoned to age in a Wonderland that no one cares about. As I was photographing a red flower, a woman came out from the back of the house and started throwing stones at me. The sudden aggression pulled me out of my reveries and I stood perplexed, immobilized by surprise. The woman started calling me all kinds of names and kneeled down to pick up more stones. She was robust and massive, her abundant hair disarranged into a diabolic nest. She wore a somehow disjointed and tight once-black dress now faded gray from many washes. Her aim was sharp and she hit me twice, once in the left knee and once in the lower back. Unfortunately, the anemic dogs acquired an unexpected vigor and rapidly joined the attack. One of them bit me in the calf and ripped my pants. Before the third round of stones arrived I fled the scene in a combined movement of limping and trotting, protecting the lens of the camera with my hands and followed by the ferociously barking and howling dogs. Some neighbors came out of their houses, curious to witness the escape of the intruder. Finally, finding myself far from the zone of hostilities, I sat on a stone by the side of the road. On the horizon I saw a black cloud from a fire staining the sky. I assessed my wound. The dog's bite left swelling but the bleeding had stopped.

Resigned to my misfortune, I thought that if Cartier-Bresson[5] were a saint, I would make him a promise right now: to abandon forever the pretended objectivity of photography—that descriptive, neutral, archival, clinical image. After all, the optical illusion created by the wide angle and the depth of field set on infinity is not a mere aestheticism; it implies a greater-than-human hyperreality as a metaphor of divine knowledge, an image that embodies the paranoid gaze of a Protestant deity—he who with his enormous eye sees it all and puts a price on everything. I would promise to abandon once and for all every attempt to redeem the fiasco of art as science in exchange for one thing: that Cartier-Bresson in the flesh would protect me at the decisive moment when the stones begin to fall over me and the dog's teeth sink in without mercy.[6]

Queens Museum of Art
Down the Garden Path

Chapter 4
Interviews and
Project Essays

{153}

(top)
Sergio Vega
Alice's Backyard, 2001
C-print, 16 x 20 inches
Courtesy of the artist

(bottom)
Sergio Vega
Modernismo Tropical
(details), 2002
Digital prints, 70 x 180
inches each
Courtesy of the artist

Modernismo Tropical

Taking short steps to disguise my limping, I headed towards the residential area above the shantytown. I came on top of the hill into a wide avenue of puzzling, idiosyncratic features. The tallest buildings were distributed alongside as if they were in a carnival parade, but instead of dancing to the deep beat of African drums, they seemed to be swinging to the cool, smooth sound of bossa nova. Their monumental presence ostentatiously announced the triumph of modernity over the jungle.

The facades of those carnivalesque buildings were painted in pure, bright colors, with curved balconies of organic design. Some were aesthetically refined, others silly but fun, many others painful to look at. One of them was called "Building Burle Marx."[7] How come the patterns employed by the landscape architect in parks, plazas, and promenades ended up literally applied to the facade? I concluded that this tropical architecture established a dialogue with nature not in order to camouflage itself but to contend with it. In some cases, it acquired an emblematic presence that not only competes with mango trees, coconut palms, and parrots but also imitates them. Even if this extravagant degree of belief in the symbolic function of form derives from the work of Oscar Niemeyer,[8] it must have made no use of avant-gardist rupture to establish itself, since its grace relies in the deviation of high modernism towards the regional.

Thus modernist architecture went someplace else, and by forgetting Cartesian logic entered a sinuous terrain that left it under the shelter of shamanism. It is hard to tell how this detour started, whether as a formalist exercise or as the result of heat stroke. In any case, it drove architecture into a performative space, to cross-dress as animal or plant. Was I hallucinating? Or could it be that architecture in the tropics also took the sad path of unfulfilled promises that abstract thought limps along, toward the high purity of forms to end up (more often than not) cramped in some sort of metaphor? Could it be that these architects were also chased by dogs?[9]

It seems plausible that the next trend in architecture will openly embrace shamanistic strategies. After all, it has already done it in a somewhat restrained manner. In the near future we may come to see a bizarre array of organic buildings acquiring the status of natural specimens. Parrot color-chart architecture, banana institutional buildings, pineapple churches, crocodilian houses, snake promenades, toucan theaters, orchid subway stations, etc. If in the process all species end up being represented, cities could become entire inventories of the natural kingdom and the whole of the modern world a monumental paradise.

When the shaman impersonates animals, speaks their tongues and emulates their movements, his actions are not just a manifestation of hysteria but the careful construction of a sign, one that indicates to the tribe that he had entered the "edenic stage." He now embodies the spirits of the animals and the plants and much more, because in that process of transformation he has gone up a ladder or a tree with a request from the tribe and is coming down with a message from the creator. However modern, a building cross-dressed as something else and presented as a message from above is indeed an ancient idea.

Observing these buildings in detail, I concluded that the materialism embodied in them has nothing to do with a dialectical logic, but it is the fruit of excess that the modern as a sign of social status acquires in the societies of the Third World. This architecture, by the mere fact of being simultaneously modern and vernacular, stands on a hybrid ground that the universalistic discourse of the canon cannot entirely name. It is the case of an architecture decidedly drunken by and sunken in the eccentricity of kitsch—a kind of unleashed, paradigmatic kitsch that submerges all of what is modernist. As a result—helped by the blurring power of time and fueled by suspicious flows of capital—it manages to generously resuscitate the modern as a parody of itself.

After photographing so compulsively, I felt tired and stressed by the heat and the pain of the bite. I limped a couple of blocks and made it to a plaza. There I finally sat on a bench to drink an orange juice. Among the trees I noticed some very large birds that seemed to be constructed of plastic. Then I noticed that people formed a line as if waiting for their turn to talk to them. These parrots—which embodied a mysterious mix of confessionals and telephone booths— had taken over the environment of the plaza and turned it into an artificial Garden of Eden. It was as if the telephone company knew that he who speaks the tongue of the animals also talks directly with God.[10]

Queens Museum of Art
Down the Garden Path

Chapter 4
Interviews and
Project Essays

{155}

NOTES

1 Parade-dancing and performing schools generally affiliated with specific neighborhoods.

2 "Mango tree."

3 "Hummingbird"; literally "flower-kisser."

4 The author establishes an analogy between the fragmentary nature of shanty constructions and the rhetorical structure of collage. If the logic of modern architecture is primarily Cartesian, the ontological condition of the shantytown is, in opposition, post-Cartesian—or of a chaos posterior to order. Its materials have been scavenged from rubbish discarded by another social class. In Spanish, the word *descarte* means to throw away, to set aside things or people.

5 Henri Cartier-Bresson (1908–2004), widely considered the most popular and influential modernist photographer. He developed the theory of the decisive moment in photography: "A velvet hand, a hawk's eye—these we should all have. . . . If the shutter was released at the decisive moment, you have instinctively fixed a geometric pattern without which the photograph would have been both formless and lifeless" (*The Decisive Moment* [New York: Simon & Schuster, 1952]).

6 The paragraph emphasizes the failure of the medium both at producing art that holds the status of scientific knowledge and as means of self-expression; in the narration, photography ends up subdued by faith (Cartier-Bresson as a saint).

7 Roberto Burle Marx (1909–1994), world-renowned Brazilian landscape architect, recognized for his paradigmatic search for biomorphic archetypes as the conceptual and structural basis for architectural design. A painter and botanist himself, Burle Marx wanted his work to create a rupture with the romantic conception of the landscape and proposed the close examination of nature from a scientific perspective. Some of his best-known projects are the park Aterro do Flamengo and the sidewalks of the Avenida Atlântica in Copacabana, both in Rio de Janeiro.

8 Oscar Niemeyer (1907–), a leading figure of Brazilian modernist architecture. His expressive style borrowed extensively from the Colonial Baroque in Brazil. From 1956 until 1964 he was chief architect of the Nova Cap Brasília project, where he designed most of the city's important government buildings (Burle Marx designed some of the gardens). These monumental buildings mark a period of high creativity in modern symbolism.

9 The author's use of narrative contiguity—since he was previously bitten by a dog while attempting to take a photograph—places abstraction in opposition to photography, a paradox in which both share a similar destiny. Based on Roland Barthes's assertion that photography is a message without a code, the unavoidable result of abstraction would be to produce a code without message. "To end up cramped in some sort of metaphor" underlines the methodological incongruence that takes place when modern architecture relies on symbolic form and undermines its functional purpose. The paragraph suggests that while postulating itself as an idealism of biomorphic archetypes, tropical architecture acquires symbolic content, or even metaphorical meaning, thus deviating substantially from the modernist concept of architectural function.

10 The author refers to the medieval iconology of the plaza as a recreation of earthly paradise. The presence of artificial parrots among tropical vegetation is interpreted as an instance in which vernacular culture secularizes medieval conceptions.

Some Garden-Writings, 1991–1994 (Partially Revised)
Thierry De Cordier

"Every day I walk in the garden and think. Sometimes, I just walk."

1

Where I live, I keep to the house.
(The way a sick person keeps to his bed.)
Since I have withdrawn to a garden, lost somewhere in the Flemish countryside, being less traceable than before—I even threw out the telephone—it has become so much easier for me to live out my thoughts.
(. . .)
Besides, I don't like to see people very much anymore. People like *speed*!
(. . .)
In this place which feeds off slowness, I find comfort in being alone and I learn to stand myself.
....

(To be sure, my wife and my two children remain an inevitable link with the outside world.)

2

In order to lean on this world I decided to leave it. As a consequence I had to provide for myself if I did not want to depend on anyone. So I thought it would be a good idea to become a gardener. Just a gardener. However, since I am such an incorrigible dreamer who spends his time scratching and scraping his own interior insatiably, I finally became a gardener in my own head.
Due to this bad calculation on my part, my wife—in order to continue to feed us—had to look for work.

3

Alone, enclosed for life in this lost garden. Never to leave it again. Live in hiding.
To vanish from sight!
This is what I aim for.
(. . .)
In the meantime, I look forward to the day when I will do nothing but piddle away my existence.
Per il loro diletto.
Come this day, I will be ready to dissolve in my own most blissful musings. No longer having to justify myself.
Ah, to be silent. As grass grows. To live as the unspoken. In any case, there is not much else to do against mod-ern life than to realize its grand futility and because of this it is probably better to be as mute as grass.
(Whereas for you out there life is just a habit.)

4

From now on, I will not let my life run its course anywhere but within the precincts of my garden . . .

5

Outside, they expect me to defend what I think, how I think, even if I think nothing or even if I have withheld my judgment in regard to things.
All this is over now, as I no longer leave here, no longer feel I have to justify why I think one thing or why I don't think one thing or why I don't think at all. In any case, the justification of a thought does not reside in the simple fact that one pronounces it or writes it down, but in the behavior or acts that ensue from it; nay, even ultimately in "no act at all."

6

Today was a perfect day!
(Nothing happened.)

7

It is noon. I am sitting at a small table at the far end of my garden, right under the sick, thin-leaved oak whose shade nevertheless keeps me out of the blistering sun.
"What a day for a daydream" (*Lovin' Spoonful*).
All over my tiny retreat waves of brambles snake their way through the thick undergrowth. Hovering over this wild nature are fat dung flies, wasps, busy bees, and all kinds of vermin making their characteristic motor-like noises. In order to protect myself against a possible bug bite, I put on a pair of long black women's gloves and I cover my head with an old widow's veil that belonged to my mother. To fool the insects I have covered some branches with strawberry jam . . . My plan works!
Then I go on staring aimlessly at the countryside.
Not that there is anything much to see from this *point of view*, but pensiveness often lures me to this secluded corner.
(My mind was so much tampered with when I was young that I have nothing left now but the imagination.)

Queens Museum of Art
Down the Garden Path

Chapter 4
Interviews and
Project Essays

Partial view of the back garden
in Schorisse, Belgium, where
Thierry De Cordier lived between
1988 and 1997. Barely visible
on the left side—dissimulated
behind the smoke—the front of

his Futurist writer's cabin.
Photo by the artist.
Courtesy Marian Goodman
Gallery, New York

8

If, for example, I decide to spend an entire afternoon in the garden just to think, I always do it so that it helps me "in practice" to get through life a little better. Thus, only to spend an entire afternoon in trying how to live a little bit better is in itself already a *savoir-vivre*.

9

The sun shines over the garden.
It is one of those moments when I find myself wondering what really goes on behind the hills that surround me . . .
I don't really know.
From time to time I listen to the news on the radio. People who drop by bring me other news. However, I am always reluctant to believe what I'm told.
Also I sometimes ask myself if the truths that I believe in here are necessarily the same as those that are upheld on the other side of the hills that surround me . . .
I don't really know.
(. . .)
In spite of everything, I admit that in this place I am far from having an all-embracing vision. I am not at all abreast of what happens in the world, not even in my own little village. Maybe I want things to be this way and I certainly do not want to learn from others what happens elsewhere. From others, I want to learn as little as possible. News is so easily distorted that in the end I prefer to know nothing.

10

When I came to live in the country, it was because of this abandoned garden. Moreover, I was tired. (A demanding social life's fatigue.) And so, in fleeing, I joined the *Great Solitaires*. In fact, I was convinced that the remainder of my life could only be lived after a drastic break.
(. . .)
Thus, I spend my days recovering from life.
Getting used to it, say.
Meanwhile, to keep myself busy, I work a little in the garden. Or turn around in circles. Occasionally, when it rains, I jot down a few lines.
Quite simply, I dissolve . . .

11

Stationary
As a tranquil gardener sitting in his hut, nailed to a chair to a table to a piece of paper to a small window to a bit of garden—I live and wonder

12

I look wearily out of the wide-open window and listen to the foliage of the pear tree rustling in the evening breeze.
—"Yes, this is it!"
The possible relationship between a pear and me is about the only thing that still interests me in this ridiculous being on earth.

13

I like to write, as I like to garden. Yet it is true, I do not spend much time on it. Sluggish as I am, I let things go by. As unkempt as my thoughts are is my garden. And in that garden, there is me again. And so on. In a way, I go back and forth between two gardens.
(. . .)
So both are poorly kept. They are not nice to look at, as one says about a well-kept garden: How nice! Whenever I work in either one, I work in parts only. I scuffle about and for a long time I was convinced that one day I would master both. Later, I understood that nothing would come of it.

14

Since my retreat to the Flemish countryside—or at least to what is left of it (so little, in fact, that living here is somewhat illusory)—I spend most of my time pacing round and round in my garden. I do not listen to other people very much anymore and I go to bed early.
Also, I surprise myself by not thinking anymore the way I used to. Not thinking the way I was taught to. Almost as if I grew tired of it with the passing years. To no longer think towards others. As if I had to think together with them, like them. No, right now I think without saying anything and take care that my thoughts are not known anymore. For it was when I realized the unbearable lightness with which most people treat someone else's thoughts that I wound up deciding not to have any thoughts at all anymore. Or at least to feign that I don't. And even if it comes out that I kept one, there is no way that I would let it leave the garden.

15

At the beginning of the week I had an enormous gate installed at the edge of my property. The gate is ridiculously big and completely out of proportion with the size of the garden. It is wrought iron with some curves and lacquered black all over. In the middle I hung a sign that says: NO TOURISTS!

Queens Museum of Art
Down the Garden Path

Chapter 4
Interviews and
Project Essays

{159}

16

I see no one.
My days are wonderful.

17

I had 22 years behind me and I had nausea when I relieved myself abruptly of the conviction (inflicted throughout my childhood) that I had to adhere to a faith and its rules in order to live my life correctly. Today, this deliverance—which was a very confusing and difficult experience at the beginning—brings me an astonishing philosophical release. I might add that in comparison to my childhood life is working out quite well for me now. Also, I no longer have to fear that anything could ensnare me in doctrine ever again. I am completely immune.

(…)

Now it is my garden—my godless garden—that guides my spirit quite well. My understanding of man's place in the world stems only from this "little patch of nature" which in all its constant variations (with the seasons) remains one and the same thing. For instance, when one morning—on rising—I first saw it under a thick blanket of snow, I still recognized it immediately as my garden.

(…)

So, if for the sake of comparison I were to apply to myself the idea of "the variable invariable" or of "the invariable variable," I would notice that actually there is not much difference. Although I behave differently according to my mood or my dressing or the phase of the moon, I am still one and the same person.

So what am I looking for? You could say somehow to attain a state of indifference. I mean indifference *between* things. As if I pretended that my behavior were equivalent to my neighbor's. As if there were no real differences between him and me other than a difference of perception. Knowing this alone affords me some peace.

(…)

On the way to apathy (in the pyrrhic sense of the word) but still distinctly embarrassed by some vestiges of guilt, I advance slowly towards the point where I fear there is no more reasonable communication.

18

Here, in the country, I hardly go anywhere anymore. I hardly think anymore either. Or at least nothing that could interest anyone else. Here, alone, I live with the lowest possible expectation. Waiting for the great nothing.

19

Beyond my garden there is nothing but confusion. As soon as I leave my garden I turn into nothing but confusion myself.

20

It is almost 11 a.m.
I sit at the long table under the pergola with the abundant bunches of grapes.
There is no one.
I am topping and tailing green beans onto a piece of newspaper. Dedicating myself to this banal task, I look at the garden. It occurs to me that in the few years I have been living here I have deliberately emulated my garden just as I have worked to make it emulate me; having merged with my garden I now mean nothing without it. At present, only this little piece of nature commands my existence. And I am so wrapped up in it that as soon as I leave, even if it is just for an hour—to go to the village, for example—straight away I feel the uneasiness of an uprooted person who has but one desire, to go back home as quick as possible. It is almost as if I need to find a way to take my garden with me in order to rekindle the desire to leave this place. If only I could somehow carry it on *my back*. Imagine …

(…)

Here, in the refuge of this garden, I narrowly escape the vainglorious tumult of the world and its 10,000 things. Little by little my life is finally becoming what I always hoped it would be; an existence of pure reticence. A moderate existence, almost insignificant, in which nothing, or not much, happens. No adventure. A human life of no interest …

Thus, yielding to this garden where I live discretely and in relative harmony with what little there is around me, I think somehow I am more or less getting my life together.

21

I light a little cigarette and say to myself that after all I have absolutely nothing to do with the twentieth century.

Translated by Frank Albers and Bernard Dewulf.

Mark Dion: *The Tasting Garden*
Robert Williams

Mark Dion's *The Tasting Garden* was one of the few permanent artworks made for Artranspennine98.[1] The project makes use of a set of hidden walled gardens to the rear of the Storey Institute in central Lancaster, England.[2] Planned by Dion as one of his trademark community-oriented projects, following in strategy and organization earlier works such as that with the Chicago Urban Action Group in 1993,[3] *The Tasting Garden* has now become a place of tranquillity beloved of Lancastrian citizens, despite a controversial beginning.[4] The project sought the involvement of many individuals from the city—youth workers, art students and volunteers, professional artists and craftspeople, landscape gardeners, architects, and others to share in its planning, building, and development.

Central to the concept of *The Tasting Garden* is a critique of global agribusiness, in this case the promulgation of fruit types that satisfy requirements of shelf life, appearance, and unit turnover rather than those of taste, diversity, or ecological significance. However, it would be a mistake to assume that the garden exists only as a polemic. Rather, it has become, in real terms, a repository of biological diversity that allows for a full experience of represented fruit types, including visual, tactile, olfactory, and of course taste dimensions: Visitors are invited to eat from trees planted next to bronze sculptures that depict the fruits those trees bear. The model for the layout of the garden refers to the various "trees" inherent in taxonomy, or in scientific and spiritual models such as those of Kabbalistic tradition or nineteenth-century phylogeny. "Trunk" and "branches" are laid out in red gravel paths. At the terminal of each branch we find either an oversize bronze fruit on a plinth next to a tree of that type or a gravelike stele with the name of a fruit type now extinct, such as "Greaves Wonder," "Green Balsam," and "Ambrosia," which the world will never see—or, indeed, taste—again. In this, the tree motif presents the Tree of Knowledge as a preserved and forbidden knowledge. The sculpture and stele, commemorative and memorial, provide classical references to the sepulchral monuments of Greece and Rome.

Hidden within the bounds of the garden, in view of ancient Lancaster Castle, lies a small, stone-built vernacular building. This is the place of the Arboroculturalist, a semimythical and unseen tree gardener. Despite his physical absence, a guiding and nurturing intelligence is implied by the tools, books, goods, and chattels contained in the Arboroculturalist's house, which, *Marie Celeste*-like, lie dust coated—relics of husbandry numinous in their obscurity. *The Tasting Garden* exists on many levels: as an environmental museum, a cultural space to project interpretation and fantasy, a pleasure garden to excite the senses, a receptacle for mysteries, and a place of contemplation.

NOTES

1 Artranspennine98 was, at the time, the largest public art project in Western Europe. The event was directed jointly by the late Robert Hopper of the Henry Moore Sculpture Trust and Lewis Biggs of Tate Liverpool. As its title suggests, Artranspennine98 spanned the central range of hills, the Pennines, that divides the west and east of the north of England, with public sculptural installations in towns and cities such as Liverpool, Newcastle, Hull, Manchester, Leeds, and of course, Lancaster—the extreme northwestern extent of the project boundaries.

2 The garden is maintained by Storey Arts and Lancaster City Council. The Storey Institute was created and covenanted as a place of art and education in the mid-nineteenth century by Thomas Storey, one of two controlling industrialists in the city (the other being James Williamson, Lord Ashton), and remains so to this day. It boasts one of the finest purpose-built Victorian galleries in the UK and, as an artist-run space, continues to show the work of living contemporary artists.

3 Dion makes a practice of inviting the involvement of groups of local inhabitants to participate in projects that impact on their public spaces. See Hal Foster, *The Return of the Real* (Cambridge, MA: MIT Press, 1996), 197; Gilda Williams, ed., *Mark Dion* (London: Phaidon, 1997), 83; and, for later examples, Robert Williams, "*Disjecta Reliquiae*: The Tate Thames Dig" in Alex Coles, ed., *Mark Dion: Archaeology* (London: Black Dog Publishing, 1999), 72.

4 There was initially some vocal opposition from local environmentalist groups who misunderstood the project. This was taken up by the Lancastrian media. The opposition rapidly dissipated, however, when the objectors became aware of the project's context and strategies through events and meetings held at the Storey Institute during the summer following the creation of *The Tasting Garden*. Those who opposed *The Tasting Garden* in 1998 are now among its staunchest supporters in the city.

Queens Museum of Art
Down the Garden Path

Chapter 4
Interviews and
Project Essays

(left)
Robert Williams
Swan's Egg Pear, 1998
Graphite on paper,
33 x 23 ½ inches
Courtesy of the artist

(top right)
Robert Williams
Lord Suffield Apple, 1998
Graphite on paper,
33 x 23 ½ inches
Courtesy of the artist

(bottom right)
Robert Williams
Ribston Pippin Apple, 1998
Graphite on paper,
33 x 23 ½ inches
Courtesy of the artist

{161}

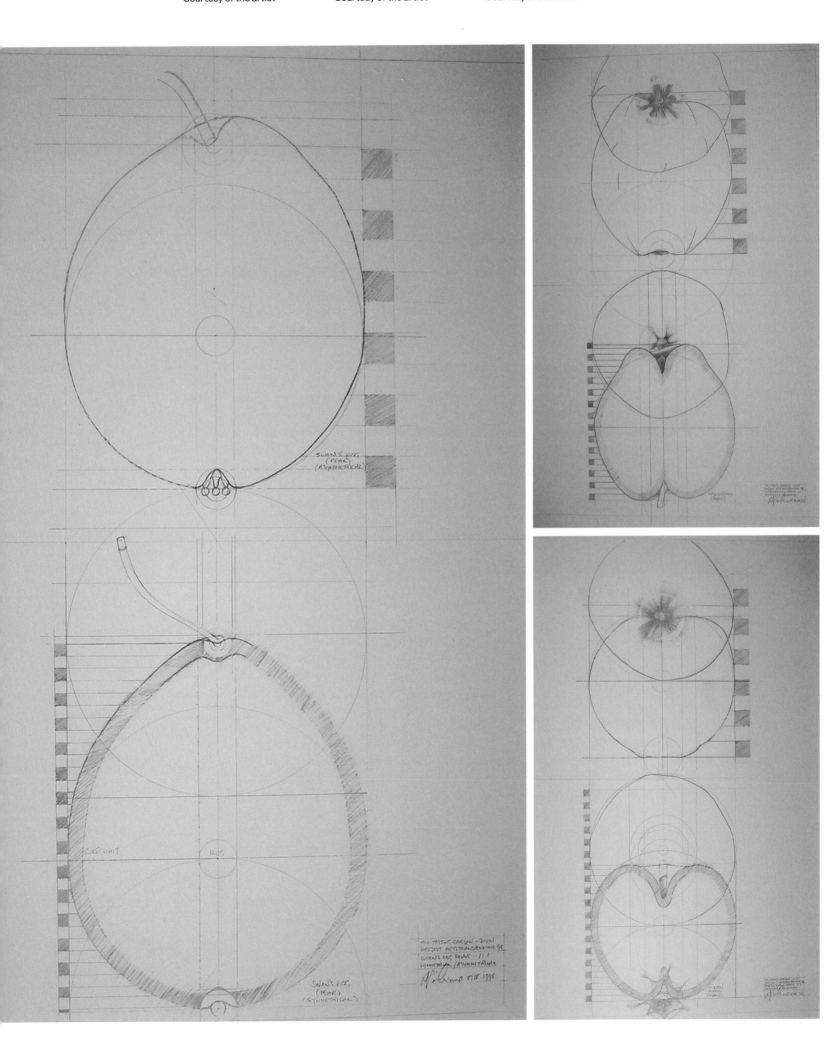

The Garden as "Art":
The Imaginary Gardens of Jan Vercruysse
Paul Geerts

"I don't design gardens because of a particular fascination or because I love them. My interest in gardens originates in art," explains Jan Vercruysse. "The drawings came about following a discussion concerning the possibility and the relevance of installing contemporary works of art in parks and market squares. I think that most of these works are not appropriate. These garden designs are my response. They are also public and create a feeling of pleasure and beauty, whereas many contemporary sculptures installed in public places have an even more alienating effect on people who are already alienated."

Real Gardens

Garden as art. But art with a strong connotation of "garden." For example, Vercruysse specifies the garden sizes, the plant names, the hedge heights, the materials used for ponds and paths . . .

"The drawings are in themselves works of art. The aim is to realize them on the ground, to really plan them. This was the goal from the start. It was not only about the creation of images."

Unlike prints from previous periods, in which existing gardens are shown in perspective, often with people moving about, Vercruysse's designs are limited to a two-dimensional picture.

"The graphic representation of existing gardens are documents concerning their look, the way people walk about them, the way they are dressed. . . . Even when those prints represented fictitious gardens or embellished reality, they were used mostly as documents and, as such, gave a picture of the period in a documentary fashion. That is not what I want. My gardens are fictitious, because they do not exist today. If I had to draw people in my gardens, how would I dress them? I should draw them naked. . . . Every time a garden will be created, it will be filmed or photographed. It will be the subject of a documentary, like these prints but with current technology."

Genius Loci

One of the principles of garden architecture is that a garden must try to express the specificity of a determined place, the genius loci. To a landscape architect, the garden is created in relation to the environment, to the house, perhaps in function of certain distinctive characteristics of the grounds, the existing trees. . . . With few exceptions, Vercruysse's gardens are conceived without any relationship to a concrete place. It's as if he began with a blank page.

"I am not involved with garden architecture. My gardens are works of art. They are not intended to integrate into the landscape. They exist clearly on their own. They add something to the landscape. I am not worried that they should be judged as being very artificial. The only question I ask myself before I start drawing a garden is to know whether it must be hospitable or not, hard or soft, quite closed or more open, simple or complex. I begin with a kind of feeling that it must evoke.

"As an artist, I am concerned with space. I modify the space, I make it visible or experiment with it in other ways. Landscape architects say the same thing. But they are dealing with applied art, which is totally different. There is an important difference between them and me: I do not have to take anything or anyone into account."

Beauty, inspiration, magic, fascination, enchantment, serenity, tranquility, intimacy, and a sense of the marvelous. These are exactly what Vercruysse's gardens convey.

Hortus Conclusus

"For many years, we have been under the spell of a certain wave of dogmatic 'leftist' thinking, full of restraints. . . . Beauty, for instance, was considered bourgeois. According to current doctrine, art must be an expression of the society in which we live. If it is ugly, so must art be ugly. There cannot be a conflict. On the other hand, my gardens want to express that conflict."

Sheltered from the outside world by high hedges, Vercruysse's closed gardens reference—maybe unconsciously—the archetype of the garden as an enclosure, a place of calm and silence, of order and sensual delight in a chaotic and antagonistic world. Similar to the medieval hortus conclusus, which existed because of a hostile outside world of violence which was to be negated, the gardens of Vercruysse are cut off from the outside world and exist as "introverted" space.

"But they are 'aware' of this world, otherwise I would not be as preoccupied by this confinement," insists the artist. "Gardens in which rooms are conceived for meditation refer, for instance, to a 'malevolent' world that does not allow for meditation or contemplation. On this level, I certainly respect a tradition, even if it was not my explicit intention."

Queens Museum of Art
Down the Garden Path

Chapter 4
Interviews and
Project Essays

Jan Vercruysse
*Labyrinth & Pleasure Garden
no. 4*, 1994
One of thirteen lithographs in
clothbound portfolio (2002),
25 ⅞ x 19 ⅜ inches
Courtesy Brooke Alexander

{163}

LABYRINTH & PLEASURE GARDEN n°4, 1994

A POND WITH A FOUNTAIN BORDERED WITH RED MARBLE, IN A CIRCULAR COURT [A]; A POND WITH
GOLDFISH, BORDERED WITH BLACK VEINED RED MARBLE [B]; A GARDEN WITH A BED OF STRAWBERRIES [C],
A BED OF WHITE ROSES [D] & A BED OF RED ROSES [E]; A GARDEN WITH TALL GRASSES [F]; AND A GARDEN
WITH TWO LAWNS WITH NO FLOWERS AT ALL [G].

A tradition that, as he rightly emphasizes, must not be at all regressive but is, on the contrary, quite progressive. Nietzsche wrote already in 1882: "Some day, probably very soon, we shall need what our big cities are missing: some very peaceful, spacious places to meditate, places . . . cut off from outside noises and street criers, . . . new buildings and plantings which together express the importance of meditation and exclusion. . . . We want to see ourselves transformed in stone and plant. We want to travel inside ourselves when we are strolling about those gardens."

In a recent book by Rob Aben and Saskia de Wit (*De omsloten tuin* [The Enclosed Garden; 010 Publishers, Rotterdam, 1998]), the enclosed garden is represented as a model to inject new life into urban and landscape projects. The inevitable growth of the city and the shrinking of the country that follows can be compensated for by a kind of surgical, small-scale intervention, introducing into the city the experience of space and landscape by means of small open spaces. With the growing attention lavished on public urban space, there is, paradoxically, a risk of creating too many spaces and parks; to witness quantity win over quality. In each new neighborhood, one "green space" or another is mandatory. But Aben and de Wit question this necessity. Should we not be more parsimonious with space, instead of wanting to impose arbitrarily squares and gardens all over?

De Wit and Aben believe that "enclosed gardens can function as catalysts on the environment. Small public spaces well conceived and carried out, in the right places, have an impact similar to acupuncture, more significant than the site. In an era where all corners of the planet have become accessible, where the computer opens up worlds with infinite possibilities, surplus, speed, and information appear to dominate the community. The areas outside of this sphere of influence are at first sight irrelevant, but in their apparent lack of interest, they could be a counterpoint for a frenetic world. To offset the acceleration, a tactic of slowing down comprised of oases of rest and peace are deemed essential."

Hortus Ludi

Jan Vercruysse also revives the idea of garden as *hortus ludi* active from the Middle Ages to the Renaissance. The "garden of delights," a profane interpretation of paradise, yields to the game of love, rhetoric, philosophy, poetry. "My gardens are contemplative gardens, philosophical gardens, where you can stroll, rest, chat a little, think, dream," says Vercruysse. He repeats almost literally what Justus Lipsius wrote four centuries ago in an essay about stability amid general disaster: "Such are the real uses and aims of a garden: rest, seclusion, isolation,

thinking, reading, and writing, all in a relaxed and playful atmosphere."

Things that appear to be generously scattered, such as ponds, stone benches, gazebos, flower beds . . . are in reality placed in a scenographic composition. Any change in the garden triggers the sequence of scenes. Perspectives and relationships are linked to movement, to a sitting or standing position. Perusing the garden should provoke thinking, study, and friendly encounters: The path toward the self, toward the other, toward the world should be traveled leisurely, step by step, along with our developing thoughts.

Various gardens have a labyrinthine structure or include requisite passage through a labyrinth to enter the pleasure garden. Vercruysse admits, "The labyrinth fascinates me not because of its symbolic, metaphoric, or erotic connotations, but simply for its shape as a graphic element. My labyrinths are not traditional. One does not get lost in them. My goal is neither to provoke people nor to torment them. Actually, they are walking-gardens made to be discovered while idling about. I am only fascinated by the physical experience and the aesthetic pleasure of walking through a labyrinth."

The artist leaves nothing to chance. He is not satisfied with giving merely the width of the garden path, the height and length of benches, or the color of the flowers. In addition, the descriptions under each plan give very precise directions concerning the elements' functions, somewhat like a storyboard. The phrase "a reading and conversation garden" recurs often. "One high pink granite bench for lonely lovers," "stone benches for conversation of a kind," "two stone benches for feeling lonely," "a garden for triangular conversation," "a circular garden with three benches for radial conversation," "a bench for no conversation at all," "a very large stone bench for multiple conversations" . . .

"I am not interested in small gardens created for sitting in an armchair under a tree or lying in the grass. My gardens are theaters. I am the director or the author who defines the roles. This is not exclusive of the fact that those who come to my gardens are free and can use them judiciously." The garden is not used as a backdrop but forms an essential element of human behavior.

Vercruysse also plays with the spectator. Not only does he prescribe the way the gardens have to be used, preferably with a partner or in solitary contemplation, but the designs of some gardens also have clear sexual connotations, such as a penis, a vagina, breasts, or an undulating spermatozoid.

Materials and shapes seem familiar to us at the same time that their artificial characteristics or extreme abstraction intrigues us. The gardens are

Queens Museum of Art
Down the Garden Path

Chapter 4
Interviews and
Project Essays

{165}

close to still lifes in that, through an insatiable desire for beauty, they illustrate in their appearance the big void and absence. Like flower beds composed exclusively of red and white roses, "a garden with an artichoke field," "a garden with two lawns and not one single flower," or "a pond with goldfish and a few aquatic plants" and "a pond with aquatic plants and a few goldfish."

Trees are scarce. In a few gardens there are magnolias or camellias but they must be pruned so they remain low and grow in width. In another, he has planned a few pots with citrus fruits ("only to make marmalade") or, again, an araucaria. He does not, however, use any tree that would grow to full height and beauty. "I do not want gardens to be dominated by a tree. On the other hand, I plant many hedges that either close or leave spaces open. They too are vertical. A tree would obstruct; one would bump into it, in all meanings of the word."

* * *

Vercruysse's gardens are not destined to be romantic representations of a natural paradise. They are spatial constructions, sculptures, in which the subject is more or less the garden.

In spite of the fact that they are totally different, they are in a way comparable to the gardens of Japanese-American sculptor Isamu Noguchi (1904–1988). For Noguchi, a garden is a sculpture of space, a total sculpture that goes beyond the sum of its distinct elements. Noguchi writes that "the dimensions and the shape of each element taken separately depend entirely on those other elements and on the given space. . . . The one who enters into it must feel that the space is at his scale, that it is authentic. An empty space does not have visual dimensions and meaning. Scale and meaning are created when a line or a set object is placed in the space."

At a time when garden architecture is overly limited to "greening" streets and squares and creating small picturesque tableaux, Vercruysse's poetic vision, his dream of a more beautiful world and his consideration of history and tradition, pose an exciting confrontation.

© Paul Geerts, 2003

Extracted from Paul Geerts, "Le jardin en tant qu'art. Les jardins imaginaires de Jan Vercruysse," Les Jardins d'Eden (Schoten, Belgium), no. 18, 2004. Translated by Claude de France with Valerie Smith.

Chapter 5
More Gardens

With every exhibition, there are ideas that arrive at the last minute, artworks that come to mind too late to treat in full. In the pages that follow, we make a playful effort to include works that take us in other directions and expand yet further the perimeters of art and the garden.

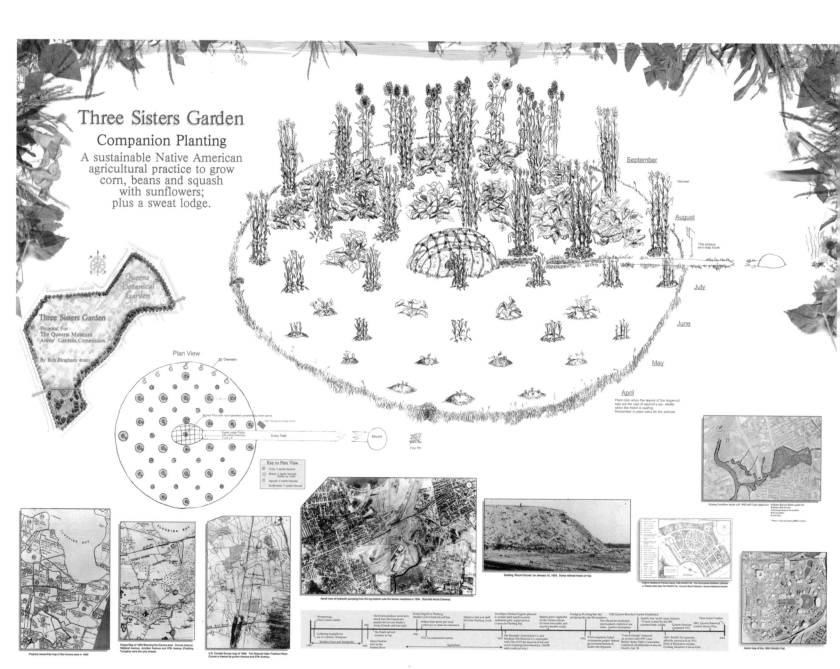

Queens Museum of Art
Down the Garden Path

Chapter 5
More Gardens

Jeronimo Hagerman

Smell-Garden Beds, 2004
Plastic mats, plastic bags, basil,
rosemary, epasote, mint, spear-
mint, geraniums, and cedron
Installation views, roof garden,
Sala de Arte Público Siqueiros,
Mexico City
Courtesy of the artist

{169}

Janet Hodgson
and Anna Douglas

The Text Garden, 1998
Topiary text in clipped yew
Aerial view, Artranspennine98,
Calderstones Park, Liverpool
Courtesy of the artists

Queens Museum of Art
Down the Garden Path

Chapter 5
More Gardens

Nancy Holt

Wild Spot, 1979-80
Wrought iron and wildflowers
(details), 10 feet diameter
Wellesley College, MA
Courtesy of the artist

{171}

Niek Kemps

(top)
Verborgen Museum I
(Hidden Museum I), 1993
Digital image
Project for a large forest with
castle and castle garden,
Ommen, the Netherlands
Courtesy of the artist

(bottom)
Verborgen Museum II
(Hidden Museum II), 1996
Digital image
Project for the Van
Abbemuseum, Eindhoven,
the Netherlands
Courtesy of the artist

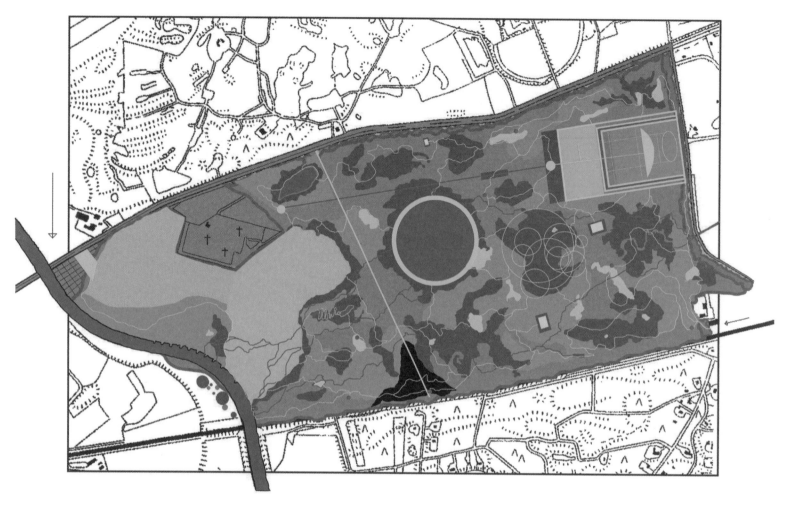

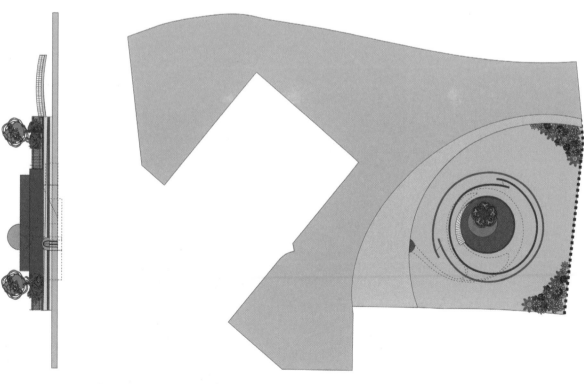

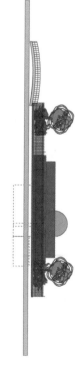

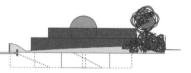

Queens Museum of Art
Down the Garden Path

Chapter 5
More Gardens

Joseph Kosuth

Ein Schiller Labyrinth, 1993
Universität Hohenheim, Germany
Aerial view and detail
Courtesy of the artist

{173}

Brian Tolle

*For the gentle wind doth move
Silently, invisibly.*, 2004
Installation view, Mall B, Cleveland
Sponsored by the Cleveland
Mall Plaza Beautification Fund,
Cleveland Public Art, the City
of Cleveland, and ParkWorks
Courtesy of the artist

Vedovamazzei (Stella Scala and Simeone Crispino)

*Go Wherever You Want,
Bring Me Whatever You Wish,*
2000-2004
Truck, water, rubber, plants,
boat, oars, wood, and aluminium,
13 x 55 x 8 feet
Courtesy of the artists and
Magazzino d'Arte Moderna, Roma

Queens Museum of Art